Set design by Paul Owen
Photo by Richard Trigg

A scene from the Actors Theatre of Louisville production of *God's Man in Texas*.

GOD'S MAN IN TEXAS

BY DAVID RAMBO

DRAMATISTS
PLAY SERVICE
INC.

GOD'S MAN IN TEXAS
Copyright © 2001 (Revised), David Rambo
Copyright © 1998, David Rambo

All Rights Reserved

CAUTION: Professionals and amateurs are hereby warned that performance of GOD'S MAN IN TEXAS is subject to payment of a royalty. It is fully protected under the copyright laws of the United States of America, and of all countries covered by the International Copyright Union (including the Dominion of Canada and the rest of the British Commonwealth), and of all countries covered by the Pan-American Copyright Convention, the Universal Copyright Convention, the Berne Convention, and of all countries with which the United States has reciprocal copyright relations. All rights, including professional/amateur stage rights, motion picture, recitation, lecturing, public reading, radio broadcasting, television, video or sound recording, all other forms of mechanical or electronic reproduction, such as CD-ROM, CD-I, DVD, information storage and retrieval systems and photocopying, and the rights of translation into foreign languages, are strictly reserved. Particular emphasis is placed upon the matter of readings, permission for which must be secured from the Author's agent in writing.

The stage performance rights in GOD'S MAN IN TEXAS (other than first class rights) are controlled exclusively by DRAMATISTS PLAY SERVICE, INC., 440 Park Avenue South, New York, NY 10016. No professional or nonprofessional performance of the Play (excluding first class professional performance) may be given without obtaining in advance the written permission of DRAMATISTS PLAY SERVICE, INC., and paying the requisite fee.

Inquiries concerning all other rights should be addressed to Harden-Curtis Associates, 850 Seventh Avenue, Suite 405, New York, NY 10019. Attn: Mary Harden.

SPECIAL NOTE

Anyone receiving permission to produce GOD'S MAN IN TEXAS is required to give credit to the Author as sole and exclusive Author of the Play on the title page of all programs distributed in connection with performances of the Play and in all instances in which the title of the Play appears for purposes of advertising, publicizing or otherwise exploiting the Play and/or a production thereof. The name of the Author must appear on a separate line, in which no other name appears, immediately beneath the title and in size of type equal to 50% of the size of the largest, most prominent letter used for the title of the Play. No person, firm or entity may receive credit larger or more prominent than that accorded the Author. The following acknowledgment must appear on the title page in all programs distributed in connection with performances of the Play:

World Premiere in the 1999 Humana Festival of New American Plays
at ACTORS THEATRE OF LOUISVILLE.

SPECIAL NOTE ON QUOTATIONS

Some Bible quotes in the Play are taken from the *Holy Bible, New International Version* in accordance with the published permission guidelines. Other Bible quotes are taken from the Cambridge University Press edition of the *King James Version of The Bible*.

Scripture taken from the HOLY BIBLE, NEW INTERNATIONAL VERSION®.
Copyright 1973, 1978, 1984 by International Bible Society.
Used by permission of Zondervan Publishing House.
All rights reserved.

The "NIV" and "New International Version" trademarks are registered
in the United States Patent and Trademark Office by International Bible Society.
Use of either trademark requires the permission of International Bible Society.

*for Ted Heyck,
a remarkable Texan*

AUTHOR'S NOTE

GOD'S MAN IN TEXAS is a work of fiction, rooted in the truth that the succession of a leader of any large organization — especially a megachurch such as my fictional Rock — rarely goes smoothly. Egos, suspicions, legacies and reputations are at stake. Not every CEO stays on top; princes who become kings may abdicate their thrones; school superintendents often forsake administrative offices to go back to classrooms and do the work that is most in their hearts.

This is a fluid play; directors should avoid blackouts between scenes. Transitions can draw on the rich lore of church music for appropriate, or even ironic, effect. The simpler the design of the production, the greater Rock Baptist Church will seem to the audience. I especially caution against the impulse to use video monitors to simulate the broadcast sermons. Reducing Rock to the size of a television screen — no matter how large — diminishes the scope of Rock as the audience had imagined it. The parade in Act Two needs nothing more than furiously twinkling lights and a clever sound design to be effective.

Gottschall, Jerry and Hugo, the trinity of the play, are real men, not caricatures of the colorful performers who make so much religious broadcasting hilariously entertaining. Rock is, as Hugo puts it, "the Baptist Super Bowl," and only the cream of the ministerial crop could come close to landing "the top job in the Baptist universe." Sure, these guys can breathe fire, but they shouldn't cross the line into comic stereotypes.

I am very grateful to the regional theatres that presented GOD'S MAN IN TEXAS following its world premiere at the 1999 Humana Festival at Actors Theatre of Louisville: the Warehouse Theatre, the Hippodrome Theatre, the Florida Stage, Northlight Theatre, Stages Repertory Theatre, the Old Globe, and the Alliance Theatre Company. I owe special thanks to John Dillon for his patience and wisdom with the playwright and the play as he directed the play's "Genesis" in Louisville, and to Leonard Foglia, whose Old Globe production was a "Revelation."

Amen.

GOD'S MAN IN TEXAS was originally produced by the Actors Theatre of Louisville (Jon Jory, Producing Director) in Louisville, Kentucky, on March 3, 1999. It was directed by John Dillon; the assistant director was Christopher Ajemian; the set design was by Paul Owen; the lighting design was by Mimi Jordan Sherin; the sound design was by Jeremy Lee; the costume design was by Michael Oberle; the stage manager was Juliet Penna; the assistant stage manager was Dyanne M. McNamara; the dramaturg was Amy Wegener; and the literary intern was Ilana Brownstein. The cast was as follows:

DR. JEREMIAH "JERRY" MEARS .... V Craig Heidenreich
HUGO TANEY .... Bob Burrus
DR. PHILIP GOTTSCHALL .... William McNulty

CHARACTERS

DR. JEREMIAH ("JERRY") MEARS — Baptist preacher, scholar and teacher in his early 40s. A seemingly conservative, ordinary man, he gains stature when preaching; his voice is startlingly rich and movingly expressive.

HUGO TANEY — Could be 35, could be 55, or anywhere in between, no one, including Hugo, really knows for sure. Reformed wreckage of a life full of drugs, alcohol and faithlessness.

DR. PHILIP GOTTSCHALL — Legendary figure in the Baptist pulpit, 81 years old, vibrant, passionate, stentorian, leonine, proud.

These men are Texans.

PLACE

The pulpit, the Ministers' Room and various other locations on the campus of the enormous and exciting Rock Baptist Church, Houston, Texas.

TIME

The present.

GOD'S MAN IN TEXAS

ACT ONE

Scene 1

The pulpit of the Rock Baptist Church in Houston, Texas. The pulpit is dark and deeply carved, over a century old. Dr. Jerry Mears, in his early forties, admires the pulpit respectfully. He carries himself with a slouch and a squint that, when he is preaching, slowly evaporate. But this is not his church, not his pulpit. The ordinariness of his appearance is so great that when he speaks the potency and richness of his voice are shocking. Hugo Taney, a reformed wreck of a man wearing a suit, tie, and wireless walkie-talkie headset appears behind Jerry. He could be thirty-five or fifty-five, nobody, including Hugo, really knows. Such is what a near-lifetime of drink, drugs and faithlessness can do to a soul.

HUGO. Dr. Mears, they're about to open the doors to the congregation.
JERRY. Moody preached at this pulpit.
HUGO. Yes sir, I have heard that.
JERRY. And Truett. The first time I was here, my father brought me to hear Billy Graham. He was on a sales trip to Houston.
HUGO. *(Laughs.)* Billy Graham wouldn't appreciate his Crusade being called a sales trip.

JERRY. My father's trip.
HUGO. Oh! Oh, of course! Sorry. Before I turned my life over to Christ, I did so much drugs and alcohol. Left me with only a little over half a working brain. Sorry.
JERRY. It's always so exciting to be here. I grew up listening to Dr. Gottschall on the radio, watched his first broadcast on TV. When I was an undergrad at Baylor, some of my classmates and I drove all night long many a time to be here Sunday morning and hear Dr. Gottschall preach. The campus outside looks very different now than it did back then, the way it's expanded. But here, inside … this pulpit, this sanctuary, this will never change.
HUGO. *(Listens, then speaks into his headset.)* Yeah, Dave? … Copy that. Out. (To Jerry.) Dr. Mears, I'll take you downstairs now.
JERRY. Moody, Truett, Graham, Gottschall …
HUGO. I don't want you thinking I'm completely stupid. I know Billy Graham wasn't a salesman.
JERRY. Actually, he was. He was a Fuller Brush Man.
HUGO. Billy Graham?
JERRY. At one time, yes.
HUGO. Well, if he'd stuck with it, I bet he'd have been their top guy.

Scene 2

The Rock Baptist Church Ministers' Room. The room pulses with power: English polished mahogany antique furniture, rich fabrics. A royal chamber, if you will. Hugo leads Jerry in.

HUGO. This is the Ministers' Room. Dr. Gottschall and you wait here until the stage manager gives me the word. Then I bring you both out to the church floor and you make your entrance. *(Jerry catches Hugo staring at him.)* Excuse my staring at you, but you look a lot taller on TV.

JERRY. Taller?
HUGO. On your TV shows, do you use a lower-than-average pulpit?
JERRY. No.
HUGO. Oh, man, there I go again, making dumb comments.
JERRY. That's all right.
HUGO. I wasn't all that smart before I started doing drugs and what-have-you.
JERRY. It's okay.
HUGO. The one part of my brain that's just fine is the part where I have my technical knowledge. My background's video production. I started here at Rock in TVBO.
JERRY. TVBO?
HUGO. TV Broadcast Ops. Operations. *(Hugo takes a wireless microphone and transmitter pack from his pocket.)* I need to do your audio. *(Jerry allows Hugo to wire him.)* Yeah, whenever Rock was broadcasting one of your shows from your church in Dallas —
JERRY. San Antonio.
HUGO. Oh, that's right, San Antonio. Well, whenever you came up on a monitor, all the guys in TVBO would stop what they was doing and watch.
JERRY. Oh?
HUGO. That voice. Even non-believers — some of what we had to hire back then was non-believers, this was before Gottschall College had a media production major — even non-believers in the studio would stop and listen to your voice. Praise God, what a gift.
JERRY. Thank you.
HUGO. Think of all the Fuller brushes you could have sold with that voice.
JERRY. My father was in sales. A sales trainer, actually.
HUGO. Did he have a good voice, too?
JERRY. He had ... he had a remarkable ability to enthuse people. He gave training seminars all over the country for Vite-America.
HUGO. Vitamins, and diet drinks, and what-have-you.
JERRY. Yes. When Dad spoke to a group of prospects, the excitement — it had weight, and energy, and motion. It was like ... like aftershave: cool and fluid, running over your palms, you catch it, you get some friction with it, slap it on, let it sting! That's excite-

ment! It wakes you up and says, "Go out and do something important today!"

HUGO. You are good. You are real good. *(Beat.)*

JERRY. I suppose Dr. Gottschall watches most of the tapes from other churches on the network?

HUGO. You mean does he watch your tapes?

JERRY. Mine, and anyone else's.

HUGO. Pastor doesn't watch TV at all; not his own network, or even his own shows.

JERRY. Oh.

HUGO. No time for TV. He's got the church here, three services every Sunday: the eight-thirty, then the ten o'clock — that's the one we tape to play on TV — then the eleven-thirty, which is mainly for re-takes, but we get a good crowd anyway.

JERRY. Quite a schedule.

HUGO. And he runs the college, and the Christian School, and all the programs. Meetings, meetings, meetings. Eighty-one years old! And he still studies in private four hours every morning in his pajamas, locked up alone in his library at home over on Overbrook. You been there?

JERRY. Oh, yes.

HUGO. He can read the Bible in Greek, did you know that? Greek! *(Jerry starts to respond, but Hugo indicates he's listening on his headset. Then, to Jerry:)* Audio needs you to say something, to get a level.

JERRY. "*HO EXSON OTA AKOUNEON AKOUNETO.*"

HUGO. Say, what?

JERRY. "He that hath ears to hear, let him hear." Luke, chapter 8. The original Greek.

HUGO. Oh. *(On headset.)* Ten-four, Audio. Out. *(To Jerry.)* Mrs. G.'s the TV-watcher. Ross Perot gave her a big old satellite dish for the house. She channel-surfs the Christian networks all day long.

JERRY. I see.

HUGO. And "Wheel of Fortune." She loves word games. Scrabble? If you ever get invited to Overbrook for a Scrabble game, run and hide. Run and hide! Mrs. G. plays to win.

JERRY. I know she's seen some of my broadcasts.

HUGO. It was her idea you come be Sunday night guest preacher

this month.
JERRY. Oh?
HUGO. We all do love Mrs. G. around here.
JERRY. Are you a member of her Sunday School class?
HUGO. Me? Lord, no! That class is the Who's Who of Houston. Of the whole country! She's got every oil company president in there, most of their vice presidents. Half of the top dogs at NASA. She's even got a converted Sakowitz coming now, praise God. You were talking about your Daddy, why, she's got Bucky Buckholz, the most famous motivational speaker in the world in that class.
JERRY. I know Bucky. He was a friend of my father.
HUGO. See? That's the Lord at work, bringing you and Bucky together again tonight.
JERRY. He's here?
HUGO. He's on the committee — the pastoral search committee. They're all here tonight.
JERRY. Well ... Bucky's a good man.
HUGO. He's got two hundred in his Fellowship of Success lunch group on campus. Captains of industry, up-and-comers, all of them.
JERRY. Quite a group.
HUGO. That's Rock Baptist Houston.
JERRY. The membership at my church in San Antonio doubled since RBC started broadcasting our services.
HUGO. So, what's your membership now?
JERRY. Just over six thousand.
HUGO. Here at Rock, we got more than that in our singles ministry alone. Not to make this a pissing contest.
JERRY. Well ... then, let's not make this a contest.
HUGO. I just get so nervous around famous people like you, and say the stupidest —
JERRY. *(Overlapping.)* I'm not famous, so don't be —
HUGO. *(Overlapping.)* Meeting people you'd only ever seen on TV — you must be used to it. I sure as heck am not.
JERRY. I'll admit, I was quite nervous myself recently, meeting President and Mrs. Clinton when they came to worship with us in San Antonio. *(A chill enters the room.)* Does President Clinton worship here when he's in Houston?

HUGO. He wouldn't be well-received if he did. Dr. Mears, Rock Baptist Church *is* Houston. And Houston does not care much for Bill and Hillary Clinton. George Bush on the other hand ...
JERRY. Well-received.
HUGO. Hero's welcome every time he walks in the door.
JERRY. He's here often?
HUGO. Sure, him and Pastor are close personal friends.
JERRY. George Bush — the father?
HUGO. Well, of course! I like Junior: Him and me got very similar backgrounds. But he'll never be half the leader his daddy was. We believe when the real history gets told, not the liberal-biased media version, George Bush will go down as one of the greatest presidents ever.
JERRY. He's not Baptist.
HUGO. He's a believer. And a patriot. I'm ex-Army myself. *(Jerry is fidgeting.)* You know, you got plenty of time before the service.
JERRY. I was hoping Dr. Gottschall would be here by now.
HUGO. Don't be nervous. Sometimes he runs in right at the last minute.
JERRY. *(Overlapping.)* I'm not nervous.
HUGO. You're jumpy as a baby chihuahua. Would you like me to fix you some tea?
JERRY. No. Thank you.
HUGO. Pastor always wants a fresh pot of tea handy. Mrs. G. makes sure we got a stock of Earl Grey, chamomile, some herbal ones and what-have-you. They're imported from England.
JERRY. No tea. Thanks.
HUGO. Pastor's very well-known in England. He preaches in London; and in one of their college towns, they named it the same as one of our southern cities ...
JERRY. Oxford.
HUGO. That's it. *(Pauses, listens and speaks into his headset.)* Yeah, Dave? ... Copy that. We're waiting on Pastor in the Ministers' Room ... Will do. Out. *(To Jerry, as he prepares a pot of tea.)* Big-time show business. You sure you don't want tea? Part of my job.
JERRY. *(Checks his watch.)* I think I'll get some air, collect my thoughts.
HUGO. Did you have to audition to get hired at your church in

San Antonio?
JERRY. Beg pardon?
HUGO. Well, guest preaching on Sunday nights this month — it's sort of your audition, isn't it?
JERRY. Audition for what?
HUGO. To take over for Pastor. Reverend Bissonette did real good last month. Real folksy, everybody liked him, especially the pastoral search committee. Tough act to follow.
JERRY. Chuck Bissonette was my roommate at Baylor.
HUGO. He's got a big church in Florida now.
JERRY. Yes.
HUGO. He's real tan.
JERRY. Yes.
HUGO. Looks good on TV.
JERRY. Yes.
HUGO. He said you couldn't play ping-pong worth a darn at Baylor.
JERRY. Oh? My name came up?
HUGO. They say Baptist is the first religion at Baylor, and ping-pong's the second.
JERRY. Chuck was the better ping-pong player.
HUGO. And you were the better Baptist?
JERRY. Our dorm room was full of his ping-pong trophies, little gold plastic men on top, holding a ping-pong paddle in mid-swat. I committed the unpardonable sin of asking Chuck to move some of the trophies off the bookcase to make room for a few books. As he stormed out of the room, he said, "Jerry, winners win, and losers lose."
HUGO. "Winners win, and losers lose." Can't argue that.
JERRY. So, how did my name come up in your conversation?
HUGO. His sources told him the committee was interested in getting a look at you, too.
JERRY. The only reason I'm here these next few Sunday nights is Dr. Gottschall invited me to share the word of God in fellowship with Christ and this congregation.
HUGO. Rock is the biggest and best-known Baptist church ever. We only had three pastors in 110 years. Pastor's eighty-one years old. Now, it don't take more than half a brain, which is about all I

got, to figure out that when you step up to that pulpit tonight in front of twelve hundred people ...
JERRY. Twelve hundred?
HUGO. *(Not stopping.)* ... you're auditioning for the top job in the Baptist universe. I'd be nervous, too.
JERRY. Please stop presuming I'm nervous.
HUGO. Rock Baptist Church Houston is the Baptist Super Bowl, Dr. Mears. And you're standing in God's locker room.
JERRY. I'm sorry. I forgot your name already.
HUGO. Hugo. Hugo Taney.
JERRY. Hugo, may I please have a few moments alone? *(Beat.)* Are you not allowed to leave me by myself, is that it?
HUGO. The rest room's in there. That marble, that's the real deal!
JERRY. I'm accustomed to having some time to myself before preaching, for prayer, for concentration.
HUGO. The sink and the toilet, they were gifts from Governor Connally and his wife.
JERRY. Hugo, I'm preaching without notes tonight, and I —
HUGO. Pastor never uses notes, either.
JERRY. I need a moment of quiet.
HUGO. Oh, well, I'll stop talking, if that's what you want.
JERRY. Thank you. *(Jerry tries to concentrate. Hugo clatters a tea cup.)*
HUGO. Sorry. I can't leave, or Pastor's tea won't be ready when he —
JERRY. Fine. just ...
HUGO. Do it real quiet?
JERRY. Thank you. *(Once again, Jerry concentrates. Hugo proceeds preparing a tray for the tea, absolutely quietly. He can be nearly invisible when he wants to be. Moments pass, and Jerry forgets he is not alone as he runs his message fast-forward silently to himself. Hugo, reading a tea box label, nonchalantly breaks the silence.)*
HUGO. This dang tea's a laxative. *(Before Jerry can respond, Hugo motions that he's listening on his headset.)* Yeah, Dave? ... I copy. Standing by. *(To Jerry.)* Pastor's just pulling in on Fannin Street.

Scene 3

The pulpit. The choir, congregation, organ and church orchestra conclude a rousing hymn as Dr. Philip Gottschall — vigorous, leonine, magnetic — kneels beside the pulpit, praying silently, bathed in a shaft of heavenly light from the TV broadcast-strength spotlights above. Jerry is seated just behind him, waiting his turn to preach. Gottschall rises and speaks Heavenward, his voice vibrating thrillingly with richness and drama.

GOTTSCHALL. "The unfolding of your word gives light." Psalm 119, that beautiful, beautiful hymn of praise to God's word. Tonight, we continue our study series, "Exodus: United in Faith, A Nation Prevails." We are blessed and privileged to have God's revealed word illuminated tonight by one of his most erudite and devoted servants, a fundamentalist — a true fundamentalist — Dr. Jeremiah Mears. I've had my eye on this young man since he was a puppy-faced preacher-boy at Baylor. Couldn't play ping-pong at all, but, oh, the Lord blessed this lad with an unshakable faith that recalls the most compelling preachers of our great Southern Baptist heritage. Now, over the last six months, we've welcomed a number of guest pastors from all over the country to our Sunday evening services. "Pastors on Parade," as our music director put it. *(He pauses, knowing the congregation will laugh at this.)* Consensus, with which I am proud to concur, has been that the most impressive of these visiting pastors have been those from churches situated right here in Texas. I know of none more impressive than my young colleague, from Crockett Avenue Baptist San Antonio, pastor, professor, and former president of the Southern Baptist Leadership Forum, Dr. Mears. *(Gottschall sits, and Jerry takes the pulpit. For a moment, it seems that he can't quite find his voice; he squints and slouches. Then, he begins. As his resonant, liquid voice pours forth, he gains stature and a searing focus into the congregation.)*

JERRY. The power of our Father's voice ... On one of those real-life mystery programs on TV recently, there was a young woman who had been given up for adoption at birth, and now was attempting to locate her real parents. When she was reunited with her mother, she learned her father had long since died. The young woman's tears poured forth like a desert creek following a spring storm. She said she was crying because she would never get to hear her father's voice. The power of a father's voice; so terrifying when it thunders, and so reassuring when it's a whisper ... I thought how healing it would be for that emotionally devastated young woman to be able to hear the voice of her Heavenly Father. A whisper. A gentle whisper. *(Beat.)* Who among us, though, has heard — actually heard — the voice of God? What does God's voice sound like? I asked my mother that question, and she replied, "Well, I imagine like Walter Cronkite." I challenged her on that: "Not Orson Welles? Charlton Heston?" She gave it a good deal of thought and loyally decided to stick with Walter Cronkite. God speaks to man a great deal throughout the Old Testament; there is a wonderful description in the twenty-ninth Psalm: "The voice of the Lord is powerful; the voice of the Lord is majestic. The voice of the Lord breaks the cedars of Lebanon." Power! Majesty! *(Beat.)* Has God ever whispered to man? The Bible mentions one specific occasion, yes: First Kings, chapter 9. The prophet Elijah is alone, in a cave, when God speaks to him to "stand on the mountain in the presence of the Lord, for the Lord is about to pass by." Powerful, cataclysmic noises surround Elijah: wind, then earthquake, then fire. This was not God speaking, and Elijah knew it. When God chose to speak, to call his servant back to his service, it was in a whisper. *Kol D'mamah Dakah*, the Hebrew for an almost imperceptible murmur, a quiet voice. A whisper. God's whisper. *(Beat.)* Let's look at this beautiful passage in Exodus 33, beginning with verse 7 where Moses describes "the tent of meeting" in their camp. This "tent of meeting," by the way, is not the Tent of Meeting that was the tabernacle, but another structure, on the camp's outskirts: "*Mikhutz L'Makhaneh Harkhak*" in the Hebrew, indicating very far away from camp. Far away from all the cries and shouts, and clanging, and livestock. In this "tent of meeting" God spoke to Moses, verse 11: "face to face, as a man speaks with his friend." Imagine! Hearing the voice of God "as a man speaks with his friend." A low voice? An intimate voice? A whisper? *(Beat.)* I believe some of you may be hearing that voice deep within you tonight, calling you; calling you to come home, to make things right in your heart and with God. Come. Come forward now. As God is speaking to you right now, Jesus is listening. Come. This is the moment. All your days on earth have been building up to this moment, right now, when you come forth and let Jesus be your savior. Come. He died for you. His Father is calling you. Hear his whisper. Come. Come.

Scene 4

The Ministers' Room. The service ended, Gottschall and Jerry enter. Gottschall stretches his arms outward, crucifixion-like so that Hugo can remove his microphone.

GOTTSCHALL. Eloquent preaching, lad.
HUGO. That was real fine preaching, Dr. M. Real fine.
JERRY. Thank you.
HUGO. I liked your take on that bit, talking with God like a friend, a lot better than what Reverend Bissonette did with it.
JERRY. Chuck Bissonette used Exodus 33?
GOTTSCHALL. Only a passing reference.
HUGO. I bet the committee liked what you said better. *(Beat.)*
GOTTSCHALL. Tired?
JERRY. Long day. But a good day.
HUGO. Driving all the way back to San Antonio …
GOTTSCHALL. You look more worn out than an undertaker's smile.
JERRY. For some reason, my message … every now and then, there's one that just drains everything out of you. You know …
GOTTSCHALL. Sure, sure! And you got 'em!
HUGO. They were with you, Dr. M.

JERRY. It's been a while since I spent any time with Exodus.
GOTTSCHALL. I didn't think that was one of your "sugar sticks."
JERRY. No, indeed. I've been working on it all week.
HUGO. You got 'em with it.
GOTTSCHALL. Yes, eventually. I was bit concerned at the start —
JERRY. *(Overlapping.)* Concerned?
GOTTSCHALL. This isn't a criticism, it's an observation.
JERRY. Yes?
HUGO. They like preaching that starts out folksy.
GOTTSCHALL. Dr. Mears is an accomplished academician, Hugo. A scholar. His insight into scripture is extraordinary and brilliantly informed.
HUGO. What if he starts out with a cute story, something one of his kids said that was real cute? Not so dark, like all that about the adopted woman crying her eyes out.
GOTTSCHALL. Hugo, where are the numbers?
HUGO. Not in yet.
GOTTSCHALL. Well, what is the delay? Get those numbers! *(Hugo exits quickly.)* Should have had the numbers five minutes ago.
JERRY. You said you were concerned at the start of my message …
GOTTSCHALL. I like preaching that starts off with a bang. Something that grabs 'em right off. *(He grabs Jerry at the chest in a sudden, powerful gesture.)* And holds 'em. *(He releases Jerry.)* But there are other ways to get a crowd's attention. *(Beat.)* Lad, how about you and I have a word before you drive off on I-10 West, "face to face, as a man speaks with his friend"?
JERRY. Face to face … Isn't the Hebrew for that phrase wonderful: *"panim el-panim."* It conveys —
GOTTSCHALL. Yes. You take milk in your tea?
JERRY. No, thank you.
GOTTSCHALL. No milk.
JERRY. No tea, thank you.
GOTTSCHALL. Oh. You don't care for tea?
JERRY. No.
GOTTSCHALL. You've been up to my private office before, haven't you?
JERRY. I've been to two of them, I think. One at Gottschall

College and one across the courtyard here.
GOTTSCHALL. I got a private office in the Gottschall Building — my real office — where I've had tea with every sitting president since Eisenhower.
JERRY. Clinton?
GOTTSCHALL. Except Clinton. I'd like to think whomever God brings to Rock Baptist when my time here is ended will be a pastor a president will want to join for a cup of tea. There are traditions. Don't read into anything here, I'm still healthy and sharp as a young wildcat.
JERRY. Praise God.
GOTTSCHALL. You had 'em, though. Out of all these "Pastors on Parade" through here, you're the one they really listened to. I'd give you a fidget factor of about two-point-five.
JERRY. How's that?
GOTTSCHALL. Fidget factor. Squirming, candy wrappers, yawning, scratching, what-have-you. Parkhurst, down from Dallas, he got a nine-point-nine. They weren't fidgeting, they were having spasmodic fits.
JERRY. Bissonette holds a crowd.
GOTTSCHALL. Not like you, lad. Not like you. The deacons like him, though. The committee likes him. He looks good on TV.
JERRY. Yes.
GOTTSCHALL. So, how do you think you did tonight?
JERRY. Well, I ... I ... If, as my father always said, the bottom line is the numbers ... I was gratified to see so many walk the aisle when I made the call.
GOTTSCHALL. It's all in the numbers.
JERRY. Bucky Buckholz knew my father, Marshall Montgomery Mears. He was a regional sales manager, a motivational speaker.
GOTTSCHALL. Learned at your daddy's knee, did you?
JERRY. He taught me to read from the Bible before I was two.
GOTTSCHALL. Good man.
JERRY. Dad worked for Vite-America —
GOTTSCHALL. Vitamins.
JERRY. Yes. And sometimes, when Dad was holding a recruiting seminar in our living room, I'd sit there with my Bible and read scripture along with him. He used scripture in his talks to — well,

to close his prospects.
GOTTSCHALL. Do they sell bee pollen? Ronald Reagan got me hooked on that.
JERRY. Whenever Dad was on a sales trip somewhere, some city, he'd go out on the street and share the gospel with total strangers. He was amazing, people stopped and listened, really listened to him. He called himself "Christ's rabid dog."
GOTTSCHALL. Christ's rabid dog? Meaning exactly what?
JERRY. Well, he'd sort of bite people with the gospel, so to speak. And then they became, well, carriers, so to speak, of, of …
GOTTSCHALL. Rabies?
JERRY. No, I'm not putting this very well … I guess I'm tired. But what I mean to say is that my fundamentalism, well, it's just always been a part of me.
GOTTSCHALL. Praise God. *(Jerry realizes Gottschall is sizing him up. He speaks to break the tension.)*
JERRY. Dad said Jesus was the greatest closer, ever.
GOTTSCHALL. I don't follow you.
JERRY. I'm pretty sure Dad got this from Bucky Buckholz, using the gospel as a model for sales technique. See, it all has to do with establishing credibility before closing the prospect. For instance, most of the people Jesus met and spoke to were total strangers. His ideas were going to sound terribly radical to them, so he had to establish credibility first, much in the way the car salesman needs you to trust him before he tells you that top-of-the-line sedan you admire has a $50,000 price tag.
GOTTSCHALL. The son of God was no car salesman.
JERRY. Of course. But to gain credibility, Jesus did something dramatic right off: a miracle, a healing, Lazarus, what-have-you — We can't do that. But Jesus also did something we can do. When he spoke to downtrodden, powerless people and told them, "Blessed are the meek, blessed are the poor in spirit," he was —
GOTTSCHALL. Being folksy?
JERRY. He was saying, "I know how you feel." Any good salesman since then, when the prospect is showing resistance, establishes credibility by saying, "I know how you feel" to that prospect. They sympathize, they bond. Then they close them.
GOTTSCHALL. That's either pure hogwash or outright blas-

phemy. God did not speak to man through Jesus to teach him how to sell expensive cars.
JERRY. I believe one of the reasons God sent his son to live among us was to give us a model, an ideal. Whether we sell cars, preach, or pitch vitamins, he speaks to all mankind.
GOTTSCHALL. Your daddy passed away, didn't he? No, it was something else ...
JERRY. Dad disappeared — *(Beat.)* Sales trip. I was almost sixteen. Dad got a big promotion, moved us to Dallas. The New Orleans police called one morning and said he was missing.
GOTTSCHALL. Killed?
JERRY. Just "missing." That's what they said. Last seen preaching on Canal Street for a full day and a half without stopping.
GOTTSCHALL. Never turned up? *(Jerry shakes his head, "No.")* What do you think happened?
JERRY. I think he was called. And he answered the call. *(Beat.)*
GOTTSCHALL. Your first church was just outside of Tyler, is that right?
JERRY. Tiny little country church. Fifty members when I got there.
GOTTSCHALL. Fifty. When I was growing up in Clarksville, fifty was a huge church. Huge! We worshiped with six other families in a little white church built on a stone foundation hand-cut by my Daddy. I preached my first sermon in that pulpit. I was five years old!
JERRY. Your life has been an amazing journey.
GOTTSCHALL. So they say. I don't dwell on it. Now, tell me, what did you get that first congregation of yours up to by the time you left?
JERRY. Oh, over two hundred.
GOTTSCHALL. How'd you do it?
JERRY. Well, all the usual procedures: stair-stepping, housecalls, young people's programs.
GOTTSCHALL. Did your own housecalling, did you?
JERRY. Like a rabid dog.
GOTTSCHALL. And tonight, at the largest Baptist church in the world, you preached to likely more than six times the number you left back in Tyler.

JERRY. Dr. Gottschall, I'm inordinately grateful for the opportunity to preach here at Rock this month. That pulpit, all its history, it has so much meaning to me.
GOTTSCHALL. I wouldn't give a peanut for a preacher who hasn't dreamed about preaching here. How big a church you got in San Antonio?
JERRY. Just over six thousand.
GOTTSCHALL. Six thousand?
JERRY. It's hard to get an exact number, but that's —
GOTTSCHALL. *(Charging on.)* They give you a house?
JERRY. There's a mortgage on it.
GOTTSCHALL. Is the deed in your name or the church?
JERRY. Uh, mine. My name and my wife's.
GOTTSCHALL. She didn't come with you tonight, did she?
JERRY. No, Melody's at home, with our boys.
GOTTSCHALL. Two boys, is that right?
JERRY. Yes.
GOTTSCHALL. How would you rate your marriage?
JERRY. Beg pardon?
GOTTSCHALL. You two happy? Don't fight over money?
JERRY. No.
GOTTSCHALL. "Wives, be in subjection to your own husbands."
JERRY. Yes, First Peter.
GOTTSCHALL. Melody have any problem with that?
JERRY. No, none. We're a fairly traditional Christian family.
GOTTSCHALL. Fairly?
JERRY. Quite so. Quite traditional.
GOTTSCHALL. College sweethearts, weren't you?
JERRY. We met my junior year at Baylor.
GOTTSCHALL. Did Melody take a degree?
JERRY. Yes, library science.
GOTTSCHALL. But she doesn't work outside the home.
JERRY. No. Never did.
GOTTSCHALL. That all right with you?
JERRY. Honestly, I wouldn't mind if she did, depending on the job. But she's never asked.
GOTTSCHALL. Family first.
JERRY. Always. Dr. Gottschall, my boys and my wife are more

important to me than ... than anything.
GOTTSCHALL. You make sure you bring them along from now on. Sit them right up front.
JERRY. They'd like that.
GOTTSCHALL. Let the people get to know you.
JERRY. I will.
GOTTSCHALL. Lad, you're a superstar in some circles.
JERRY. Well, I've been around a long time.
GOTTSCHALL. We've fought some battles together, haven't we?
JERRY. Always on the same side.
GOTTSCHALL. On God's side. Defending his word.
JERRY. Yes.
GOTTSCHALL. I do admire your fundamentalism. The church needs it. This church needs it.
JERRY. It's all there in the word. I just believe in the word with all my heart.
GOTTSCHALL. The word cannot be chopped up, molded, subverted to suit what passes for popular morality these days.
JERRY. No.
GOTTSCHALL. The word is not some roadside fruit stand; pick what looks pretty and tastes sweet, and ignore the rest.
JERRY. No.
GOTTSCHALL. Gotta take the sweet and the sour. You eat dried pitted prunes?
JERRY. Uh ... no.
GOTTSCHALL. Well, you should. Put some color in that pale face of yours. Folks like a pastor with good color. Keep the stuff of life moving through you, keep it moving. I'm eighty-one years old.
JERRY. Yes, sir.
GOTTSCHALL. Make a fist. Go ahead, make a fist. Now, sock me. *(Points to his stomach.)* Right here.
JERRY. No, I —
GOTTSCHALL. Punch me!
JERRY. Dr. Gottschall — No!
GOTTSCHALL. Think you'll hurt the old man? Think he's soft?
JERRY. No —
GOTTSCHALL. Hit me!
JERRY. I can't!

GOTTSCHALL. Do it!
JERRY. Pastor … *(Jerry suddenly socks Gottschall in the gut. The older man barely feels it and laughs.)*
GOTTSCHALL. Like steel! That's from two hundred sit-ups and a bag of dried pitted prunes every morning.
JERRY. You're a very healthy man.
GOTTSCHALL. And I'm going to live a long time. *(Beat.)* Did you know this pastoral search committee was convened without anybody consulting me? Not one soul thought enough of the sitting pastor to even let him know what was going on.
JERRY. Dr. Gottschall, there isn't a pastor more beloved by his congregation anywhere —
GOTTSCHALL. When God gave me this church, with all its history and all its rich and powerful people, he also gave me a vision: to make Rock Baptist the center of your life from the day you're born to the day you die. See, a baby's born, I dedicate that little baby to Christ. He's cared for in our Little Lambs day care, then our nursery school, and our Blessed Flock Sunday School. The very day they took the Lord's Prayer out of the public schools, I went out and raised the money to build Rock School for that little baby's elementary schooling, then Rock High School, and Gottschall College.
JERRY. I was in the crowd the day you broke ground for the college.
GOTTSCHALL. Now, thousands of young people come through here, learning the word of God, *living* the word of God, then going out into the world and changing lives through the word of God.
JERRY. It's one of the most inspiring —
GOTTSCHALL. *(Charging on.)* Young people spend their summers at our Camp Galilee, keep their bodies clean and fit for God's work right here in our Family Life Center gymnasium. I built that gymnasium, two swimming pools. Oh, I fought battles to build it. I had to get hold of the movers and shakers and shake the loose change out of their pockets to build it. But I built it, all of it, because I knew more and more young people and families would come if I did. Get 'em in the pool on Saturday, they'll be in a pew on Sunday.
JERRY. And they've kept on coming.
GOTTSCHALL. And coming, and coming. God gave me the

vision! You see? Every week, we tape our ten o'clock for TV and radio so that more, and more, and more can see and hear — proof persuasive as the blood-stained hands and feet of the resurrected Jesus — that this is the place to come to rejoice and be in his presence, *right here!*
JERRY. You've made this the place.
GOTTSCHALL. And when that young man, raised in Christ is ready, he joins our singles ministry and meets a pretty Christ-centered girl, they go on dates right here on campus at our dinner theater or our bowling alley. They get married, have children, and with those little babies the process begins all over again. Continuity. *(Beat.)* Continuity is very important to me.
JERRY. Yes.
GOTTSCHALL. My beloved Julia and I were not blessed with a son. We prayed on it, and prayed on it, but the Lord ... Julia is so wise about these things. When the Lord gave us our sweet Pauline, Julia said it was because the Lord knew we had the capacity to love her ...
JERRY. Mrs. Gottschall's devotion to her is inspiring to so many other parents of ... *impaired* children. *(Beat.)*
GOTTSCHALL. I got ears all over campus, all over Houston ... "The old man's mind wanders ... Memory's going ... Gets tired ... Alzheimer's ... Parkinson's ... " I've never had so much as a head cold. I've got the prostate of a man half your age! *(Beat.)* But the Lord has his timetable for all of us. I have to think about a successor.
JERRY. And the search committee's been looking for over a year now?
GOTTSCHALL. The seventh trumpet of the Lord will sound before that group of glad-handers agrees on anybody.
JERRY. Still, they'll have to eventually. Our doctrine doesn't allow a departing pastor to appoint a successor.
GOTTSCHALL. No ... That's not my intention, lad. Not my intention at all.
JERRY. Sir, am I under consideration? *(Gottschall doesn't answer.)* One doesn't like to pay attention to rumors, yet one can't help speculating. *(Beat.)* The speculation has already reached my congregation.
GOTTSCHALL. Lad, I have nothing to do with this. It's in

God's hands. We'll have to wait. *(Jerry takes a moment to carefully phrase his response. As he is about to speak, Hugo knocks and enters with a printout.)*
HUGO. I got the numbers, Dr. G. Twelve hundred and thirty-one in attendance, sixty walked the aisle. *(This pleases Jerry.)* Income: nine thousand one hundred and eighty-four dollars — that's low.
GOTTSCHALL. Leave it.
HUGO. I need to get Dr. Mears' audio.
JERRY. I put it over there.
HUGO. *(To Gottschall.)* Pastor, removing the audio is part of my job.
GOTTSCHALL. Hugo, Dr. Mears doesn't want your job. Not your job.
HUGO. Dr. Mears, next Sunday evening I'd appreciate you letting me handle your audio.
JERRY. Yes. Thank you, Hugo.
HUGO. Don't forget: folksy. Some of the committee's having punch and cookies just now, and I happened to overhear ... *(Gottschall and Jerry pay strict attention.)* They like you. But — God's truth — I actually heard Bucky Buckholz say ordinary folks liked your daddy so much, 'cause when he talked, it was like he was just one of them.
JERRY. Folksy.
GOTTSCHALL. No matter what happens, you do realize that just by bringing you here tonight, God could be working to change your life beyond your wildest dreams, don't you?
JERRY. Um ... yes. And thank you. Thank you again.
GOTTSCHALL. Not at all, lad. Not at all. 'Til next Sunday night. *(Jerry exits.)*

Scene 5

The pulpit. One week later. Gottschall sits behind Jerry, who begins his message with more than his customary unease.

JERRY. It's a pleasure to be here for a second time this month with all of you, um, nice ... *folks*. Continuing with our study series on Exodus ... Perhaps it is because I'm a parent — Melody and I have two boys, my "little men," sitting right up here in the front row. Perhaps it is because I'm a parent that in studying Exodus, I see again and again that Moses, who grew up without having a father there he could speak with, records his dialogue with God as a series of a father's commands and a son's attempts to please him by fulfilling them. Indeed, Moses himself says in Deuteronomy, chapter 8: "As a man disciplines his son, so the Lord your God disciplines you." The lesson of Exodus is that only through complete and total faith in God can we obey him completely. Wouldn't our children do what we ask, without questioning, if they honestly believed everything we tell them? For years, John, our younger boy, would not, under any circumstances whatsoever, eat broccoli. We begged, pleaded, threatened, he would not do it. We commanded. He would not obey. He may have heard about the great uproar that occurred when President Bush — the first President Bush — refused to have broccoli served in the White House. I don't know. He did, however love cooked spinach, wanted spinach with every meal. But one night, Melody decided to try serving broccoli again. As expected, John refused to eat it, and there were tears and all kinds of dramatics. Over a vegetable! Well, I'd about had enough. I told John it wasn't broccoli, it was spinach trees. I showed him the little "spinach" buds in each floret, and explained the stalk was the tree trunk — and John's been eating broccoli ever since. Isn't that right, son? *(Beat.)* So ... Enough about my family.

Scene 6

The Ministers' Room, later that evening. Hugo is on the phone, reading from a computer printout.

HUGO. Numbers are real good tonight. Income over eleven thousand — that's good for a Sunday night ... Yes, Ma'am ... Yes, Ma'am, sixty-six walked the aisle. I think they really like him, Mrs. G. And didn't he do just like you told me to tell him? Real folksy. All that about his little boy, they liked that ... Well sure, everybody hates broccoli ... Okay, hang on a minute, I'll see what's keeping Dr. G .... *(Before Hugo can put the phone down, Gottschall strides into the room, followed by Jerry.)*
GOTTSCHALL. Broccoli? What in creation prompted you to preach on broccoli?
JERRY. A parable from personal experience on obedience ...
HUGO. *(On phone.)* Here he is. *(Hands the phone to Gottschall.)* Mrs. G. From the car.
GOTTSCHALL. *(Snatching the phone.)* It was a story about how you tricked your boy into eating broccoli.
JERRY. Not "tricked" ...
HUGO. Mrs. G. thought the broccoli part was real good.
GOTTSCHALL. *(On phone.)* Hello, Beloved. I thought you were staying to join us ... *(Hugo hands him the printout and begins removing his audio.)*
HUGO. Numbers are up tonight.
GOTTSCHALL. Numbers are always up when President Bush — *the first President Bush* — is here.
JERRY. President Bush was here tonight?
GOTTSCHALL. *(To Jerry.)* Upon my invitation. To hear the brilliant young preacher we brought in from San Antonio. *(On phone.)* Well, then send the car back to my office. I'll be home in an hour. Good night, Beloved. *(Hugo hangs up the phone for him.)*
JERRY. President Bush — I had no idea.

HUGO. He's waiting in your office. I fixed a pot of Darjeeling for you and Tetley for the President.
GOTTSCHALL. Broccoli is not served anywhere on campus, did you know that?
JERRY. No.
GOTTSCHALL. We got a restaurant, a coffee shop, three snack bars, four cafeterias and a dinner theater, all serving complete, delicious meals without one stalk of broccoli. By my order!
JERRY. My message wasn't really about broccoli.
GOTTSCHALL. *(Studying the printout, to Jerry.)* Lord help 'em, they love you. *(Gottschall exits quickly.)*
HUGO. I think it was real brave of you to go for "folksy." *(Jerry allows Hugo to remove his audio.)* You're the lead candidate. Everybody's talking about it.
JERRY. That's very flattering.
HUGO. You gonna take the job?
JERRY. First of all, there is no job. Dr. Gottschall is pastor of this church, and he has not announced his retirement.
HUGO. The committee —
JERRY. The committee hasn't said a word to me. And there's no sign that Dr. Gottschall's unable to lead the church. So ...
HUGO. Okay, okay. I get it. We'll be all polite and "we're not really talking about it" and what-have-you. Let's just say Dr. G. *was* stepping down, wouldn't you take the job?
JERRY. I have a large church — large by most standards — which is the central force, if not the salvation, of the lives of thousands of people. Good, wonderful people. They've trusted me with expansion plans, fundraising, media, a multimillion dollar budget.
HUGO. Here you could get all that plus a dinner theater, bowling alley, eight-screen cineplex for family movies, Christian satellite network —
JERRY. Yes, yes —
HUGO. Restaurants, coffee shops, snack bars —
JERRY. I know!
HUGO. Full-equipped gymnasium, two swimming pools, baby care, day care, counseling center, kindergarten, grade school, middle school, high school, Gottschall College —
JERRY. Yes!

HUGO. Gift shop, book store, music store. *(Beat.)* Ballpark, football stadium, summer camp, singles ministry, full orchestra, three hundred in the choir, two marching bands, the world's biggest Christmas electric light parade they hire show people from Las Vegas to design the floats for, parking for two thousand cars —
JERRY. You don't have to —
HUGO. And my personal favorite thing on the whole dang campus: that big bowl of peppermints at the reception desk, and they're free, take all you want. *(Beat.)* Yeah, it's tempting. I know you want it. And I can help you get it.
JERRY. Oh?
HUGO. I'll do for you what I did for Reverend Bissonette and all the rest of these pastors coming through here: tell you what I hear, and what people like and don't like about you. All I want is for whoever gets the job to remember who helped them get it, and keep me on here. Because, if I'm out there, I'm dead.
JERRY. Dead?
HUGO. It's no big secret I was once a bit what you might call "wild." Wild! Saturday nights, drinking, all kinds of drugs, sex I don't half-remember with anything on two legs. And I do mean *anything*. Pretty ugly picture, but I was too drugged-up to see it that way. Sunday mornings, my poor momma would drag me out of bed and stick me in the one jacket my daddy left behind when he run off with the divorcee in the next trailer who had three breasts. I'm not making that up, she did; the extra one was halfway between her right breast and her armpit. We all seen it. Well, I'd sit there on them painful wooden benches in church, still half-stoned or hungover, Momma clutching me so I wouldn't run and hide. Surrounded by every ripe young Baptist female in town. Preacher hollerin' in the pulpit. Sweat pouring down my backbone. Head pounding. Room spinning — I up and vomited right there. The preacher and everybody yelled, "Praise God! Jesus expelled Satan from deep within this sinner's body right out on to the carpet." But after it happened a couple more times, they kicked me out. *(Beat.)* I joined the Army, turned total alcoholic, and one night in Honolulu paid fifty bucks to have "Jesus Wept" tattooed on the right side of my behind.
JERRY. Somehow you got saved and came here.
HUGO. I got a dishonorable discharge out of the Army, and I just

drifted, doing motorcycle repairs, odd jobs, video production, burglary, selling drugs and what-have-you. Over the years, I made my way back to Texas. And one night, sitting at a bar in El Paso, I heard a voice. It sounded like ... like what I remembered my daddy's voice being like. I hadn't given him a passing thought in twenty years; for all I knew he was long dead. This voice, right in this ear, so close it tickled a bit, said, "How long are you going to keep trying to kill yourself?" And I spun around like that to see who was talking — but the only people in that bar was me, and way down at the other end, the bartender, and a yellow-haired transvestite, and a crippled man trying to get free drinks by doing tricks with hard-boiled eggs and a spoon. I got sick to my stomach and shot right out the door. And right there, under a streetlight, there was a nice sort of middle-aged man preaching to a crowd. Was he excited about Christ! Man! *(Beat.)* He looked right at me, right in the eye. And he said, "God loves you. He sent his son to die for you. He won't give up on you. You have been running from Christ all your life. But you're not running any more, because I got you. And I'm Christ's rabid dog."
JERRY. Christ's ...
HUGO. Rabid dog. And he was. He would not let me go. I was so scared. Terrified. But he stayed there, praying with me, letting me cry on him and mess up his nice jacket. We talked all night, and he found out I could do video production, and he told me RBC was just getting the network up and running. He said pray, and God would provide me with a job.
JERRY. Saved on a street corner ...
HUGO. And led here, to the Rock ... of my salvation. Now, if I look down from here, I can see the Devil there in ice-cold, black water, swimming in all that evil from my wild past. Part of me wants to jump in, just for a quick dip. But I know if I do, I'll never find my way back. *(Beat.)* What do you see when you look down from your rock? A pitiful talent for ping-pong and a kid that won't eat broccoli.
JERRY. My story's more interesting than that.
HUGO. Well, Preacher, what you got to do, if you want the job, is next Sunday night you better tell 'em your story. And it better be a real grabber.
JERRY. Hugo, I've got a real grabber to tell you right now. It's about my father.

Scene 7

The pulpit, the following Sunday evening. Jerry preaches as Gottschall, seated, watches.

JERRY. Not every man who is called to preach actually hears God's voice calling to him in the manner that, say, God called to Moses over the hissing and the crackling of that burning bush. But I believe God did call me. I believe I heard his voice. *(Beat.)* From my mother I developed a love of books, and from my father I inherited a love — a passion — for the Bible. The summer I was ten years old, I made my mother drive me every week to wherever the Youth Crusade For Christ set up its tent so I could hear the preaching and compete in Bible drill. It's hot in North Texas in the summer, especially inside a canvas tent full of children. The Crusade evangelists were kind enough to offer an ice-cold snow cone on the spot to any child that accepted Christ right then and there as their personal savior. I got saved just about every week. The old "right now close": Get saved *right now* and get your snow cone, five delicious flavors! Dad thought I should have more significant spiritual guidance, so he sent me to Colt Bible Camp, outside Lubbock, started by the Colt family that made guns. The camp's motto was "Fellowship and Firearms." I got poison ivy the first day and spent two weeks in the infirmary memorizing Matthew's Gospel and learning how to clean, oil and re-assemble a .22-caliber rifle. *(Gottschall squirms.)* Shortly after I'd turned fifteen, my parents and I were sitting, one Sunday, in a blue vinyl booth at the International House of Pancakes in Forth Worth. All through church, the McAllister girl had been smiling at me from the choir, and now, here she was again, doing the same thing to me from the next booth. I recall it was very, very hot in there, and I was perspiring so much my mother thought I was ill. *(Beat.)* The next thing I knew, there was a roaring sound, the blood was rushing through the veins in my ears so fast it sounded like rapids, thundering whitewater rapids. *(Jerry steps forward, isolated in a wash of bright light as lights go out on everything else.)* I felt the whole restaurant vibrating, and then it was like the building blew away, and I was in a bright, blinding desert. I felt the hand of God come down at me, enter my chest and grab my heart, massaging it. My blood flowed through my veins not by my heart's own beating, but by the rhythmic pumping motions of the hand of God. He pulled, jerking me up on my feet. And I heard his voice: "You are mine!" *(Beat.)* And just like that it was over. I had been called.

Scene 8

The Ministers' Room, the following Sunday evening. Hugo is on the phone.

HUGO. Two hundred forty thousand the first year alone, Cadillac car, house, two secretaries … hold on, I'll find out. *(On headset.)* Hugo to Dave. You copy? … Dave, what's the deal on the office? … Ten-four and out. *(On phone.)* Mrs. G? That would be a personal customized office on the top floor of the Gottschall Building … will do. Ten-Four. I mean, goodbye … *(But she's already hung up. Jerry enters, drained.)*
JERRY. Chuck Bissonette …
HUGO. It's just a feeler offer, nothing official.
JERRY. Winners win, and losers lose. *(Jerry lets Hugo do his audio.)*
HUGO. Mrs. G's got a command post set up at Overbrook, calling the media, telling them Pastor has no plans of retiring whatsoever.
JERRY. But if the committee wants Chuck —
HUGO. Now, look, only half of the committee made that offer. Just went off and did it on their own, without telling the rest of the guys — or Dr. G.
JERRY. Half of the committee?

HUGO. They're split: half for you and half for Reverend B. It's civil war.

JERRY. Well, at least I had half of them.

HUGO. You'd have all of 'em if — Well, I hate to say it, but you're Dr. G.'s man, and that's what's working against you. Some of them don't think that's right. *(Gottschall, ashen, enters the room so silently that Hugo and Jerry don't hear him.)*

JERRY. No pastor should be able to appoint his successor. It's not Baptist tradition, not our doctrine.

GOTTSCHALL. Our doctrine wouldn't have allowed Moses to appoint Joshua as his successor ...

JERRY. Good evening. *(As Gottschall gathers steam, Hugo serves his tea, which is ignored.)*

GOTTSCHALL. Word gets out I'm bucking for to you be my Joshua, and — *snap!* — those committee boys can't get to the nearest telephone fast enough, start making deals.

JERRY. I'm flattered that you —

GOTTSCHALL. Don't be flattered. I never said who I wanted. Never said I wanted anybody. *(He explodes.)* Insubordination! I built this church! Sure as the blood from my Daddy's swollen, dusty, cut-up fingers is on every piece of foundation stonework laid in Clarksville for twenty years, the foundation of this church, this multimillion-dollar operation, has got my blood on it. And I will not — will not! — leave it in the manicured hands of some smiling, suntanned ping-pong player! I wanted to bring somebody in as co-pastor first, work with me for a brief period, an orderly transition. *(This is news to Jerry.)*

JERRY. Well, that's ... that's a wise approach.

GOTTSCHALL. *(Charging on.)* I will not have it done any other way. Will not! I'm bringing Bucky Buckholz up to Overbrook later to strategize. We'll just see who's running things around here. Hugo!

HUGO. Yes, sir, Dr. G.

GOTTSCHALL. Wire me up! We got preaching to do. *(Gottschall strides out of the room, Hugo follows. Jerry stays behind and prays.)*

JERRY. Lord, I am so confused at this moment. Why did you lead me here? Was it to test me, test my ambition, my humility? I do

confess I wanted this to be mine. I felt — I feel — that here I could serve you, proclaim your gospel and bring souls unto you in a way that is not possible anywhere else on earth. Why won't you let me do this? Am I not up to the job? *(Hugo, returning to the door, listens.)* Lord, I can't help feeling how ironic it is that my message for tonight is going to be on where — after slavery, plagues, the Exodus, receiving the Commandments — Moses asked you for a favor. He asked you to reveal yourself to his people. Not a small favor to ask. But you agreed to do it, because, you told him, "I am pleased with you." To hear your voice, to hear you say, *(Whispers.)* "I am pleased with you ... " *(Beat.)* Lord? *(Jerry listens; he listens hard and listens needfully. He hears nothing until:)*
HUGO. Dr. M., we got to get this show on the road.
JERRY. Fine. Fine. I'm ready.

Scene 9

The pulpit. Jerry sits as Gottschall preaches: a simmering volcano.

GOTTSCHALL. "When?" I hate somebody asking me when something's supposed to happen. "When?" What an utterly useless question. I do not like, I cannot abide, I will not tolerate useless questions. *(Beat.)* When somebody asks, "What time is supper? When is the next bus supposed to leave? What time does 'Wheel of Fortune' come on?" you can tell when all that's going to happen because these are *unimportant* things. If you know when something is going to happen, it is an *unimportant* thing. *(Beat.)* When Jesus was resurrected, and showed himself again to the apostles, they said, "Lord, are you at this *time* going to restore the kingdom to Israel?" Would anybody here not agree that restoring the kingdom to Israel is an *important* thing? Of course it is! And that's why Jesus told the apostles, "It is not for you to know the *times* or *dates* the Father has set by his own authority." *Important* things. In

God's time. *(Beat.)* Throughout John's gospel — you sit down and study on this when you get home, you'll see what I mean — Jesus says over, and over again, "My time has not yet come." My time. My time ... Everybody, even his mother, keeps asking Jesus, "Why can't you do this? Why hasn't this thing happened," or, "When will such-and-such occur?" Over and over, Jesus says, "It's not time." Not time. *(Beat.)* Ecclesiastes, chapter 3: "There is a time for everything." What time would that be? God's time. Read verse 17 with me: "God will bring to judgment both the righteous and the wicked." When will that happen? Well, read on: "For there will be a *time* for every activity, a *time* for every deed." That time is God's time. *(Beat.)* Do you know what day, exactly when, the Lord will take you from this life? Do you know? Can you tell by looking at your Timex watch? Of course not. That happens in God's time. Because it is an *important* thing. *(Beat.)* Jesus speaks in Revelation, "I am coming soon." When is that? When is *soon*? What year will that be? What day? What hour and minute? In God's time. *(Heavenward.)* Lord, I am ready for your coming, I'm good and ready, but when is it going to happen? You commanded us to endure patiently, and we're trying, oh, Lord, we are trying to be patient, but we've been waiting for two thousand years! When, Lord Jesus, when will judgment day come, and the glorious rapture, when the righteous are lifted up to greet you and dwell with you in the New Jerusalem for ever and ever — when? *When? (To the congregation.)* In God's time. Because these are the *most* important things. *(He digs in at the pulpit.)* I'm not going anywhere until God says, "It's time."

End of Act One

ACT TWO

Scene 1

The Ministers' Room, Sunday morning, three months later. Gottschall and Jerry enter in high spirits just after the conclusion of the eight-thirty A.M. service.

GOTTSCHALL. There's *excitement* here today!
JERRY. Yes. It went well.
GOTTSCHALL. We got a few minutes to put our feet up before the ten o'clock. *(Hugo enters, carrying a large gift-wrapped box.)*
HUGO. What a crowd! Parking lot looks like a beehive: all the Christians with them fish on their back bumpers, running each other down for parking spots. *(To Jerry.)* This was just delivered for you. *(Jerry, puzzled, takes the package and reads the card. Hugo serves Gottschall's tea.)*
GOTTSCHALL. Jerry? Tea? No, that's right, you don't —
JERRY. No, thank you.
HUGO. There must have been over forty-four hundred in there. And that's just the eight-thirty. You ought to see how super-dressed-up the ten o'clock crowd looks, like they know this is going to be the most-watched broadcast ever.
GOTTSCHALL. You want the girl to come and give your face a little color?
JERRY. No.
GOTTSCHALL. Just for TV.
JERRY. No, thanks.
GOTTSCHALL. You need a little color. Half of Texas, half the *country* tunes in for the ten o'clock. What is that?
JERRY. It's from Chuck Bissonette.
HUGO. You got time to open that before the ten o'clock.

GOTTSCHALL. Hugo, get the girl on in here.
HUGO. Will do, Pastor. *(To Jerry.)* Pastor. *(Gottschall is not used to anyone else being called "Pastor" in his church. Hugo exits. Jerry opens the box and smiles, pulling out a ping pong trophy.)*
JERRY. Winners win, and losers lose. Chuck's benediction.
GOTTSCHALL. If Bissonette hadn't been so arrogant, so greedy, so hog-like about wanting the whole thing for himself, he could have been here right now, getting ready to preach in front of what is certain to be record numbers of people watching TV — Forget the *Texas Baptist Standard*, forget the Texas papers, period. Your picture was in *Time* magazine!
JERRY. My name is news only because of your importance in the history of this remarkable church, this country, even. Jerry Mears' new job is not news. The selection of Dr. Philip Gottschall's co-pastor is news.
GOTTSCHALL. "Co-pastor ... " Well, it's always a thrill the first time your picture's in *Time* magazine. *(Beat.)* You getting any exercise?
JERRY. I keep myself pretty fit.
GOTTSCHALL. Get your heart pumping, circulation going. Color in your cheeks!
JERRY. Believe me, my heart's pumping quite vigorously right now.
GOTTSCHALL. You're excited. We're all excited for you. Why, before four o'clock this morning, Julia was already up and out of bed, fixing breakfast, getting Pauline into a new outfit. Julia's very fond of you, son.
JERRY. I wouldn't be here today if she hadn't been so supportive.
GOTTSCHALL. She — I shouldn't tell you this.
JERRY. What?
GOTTSCHALL. *(Laughing.)* Well, she ... She is something. And she plays to win, as you well know from the licking she gave you at Scrabble.
JERRY. Yes.
GOTTSCHALL. Well, she ... *(Laughs.)* You know, membership in her Sunday School class is harder to come by than membership in any country club in Houston. There's a lot of big deals have been made out of relationships forged in that class. Big deals. You

ask Ross Perot, he'll tell you. And she ... she told Bucky Buckholz to tell his committee that if they didn't quit talking to Chuck Bissonette and start talking to you, she'd kick the whole bunch of them right out of her class. She plays to win.
JERRY. I didn't know she'd done that.
GOTTSCHALL. Son, you had me, Julia, God and old George Bush on your side.
JERRY. President Bush? I'm ... I'm astonished. I was under the impression —
GOTTSCHALL. Spinach trees! He loved that, made him look at broccoli in a whole new light. In fact, a couple of days after you preached on that, he was having dinner at the Petroleum Club — Bucky was there, he told me this story, God's honest truth — and the president thought, why not try it, broccoli, see if it tasted like spinach after all. George Bush ordered broccoli! Well, jaws and menus fell all over the club. The Secret Service man about had a stroke on the spot and sent iced tea flying every which way.
JERRY. And did Mr. Bush like the broccoli?
GOTTSCHALL. Hated it. But you got him to do something his mother, his wife, and every broccoli farmer in the country couldn't do. You got him to at least give it another try. He's coming to the ten o'clock.
JERRY. I'm ... I'm honored.
GOTTSCHALL. Now, you watch Julia. She'll spoil your boys, treat them like grandkids. She'll spoil them worse than she spoils our Pauline — the boys, you, and your pretty little Melody.
JERRY. She's already got Melody on a dozen committees ...
GOTTSCHALL. Good, good.
JERRY. ... and teaching kindergarten Sunday School.
GOTTSCHALL. People are crowding in out there because they *want* to know you. The flock follows the shepherd because they know him, they know his voice.
JERRY. I want to know them, too.
GOTTSCHALL. Good, good, son. Preaching the eight-thirty every Sunday's a good start, gives you a chance to ... to —
JERRY. To establish credibility with the congregation.
GOTTSCHALL. That's right. But I want you to have high visibility on campus as well. High visibility. Mrs. Neville typed up a

schedule for you of all the events in the coming couple of weeks where you're expected. *(Finds it.)* Here.
JERRY. Did she check schedules with my secretary?
GOTTSCHALL. This will keep you out of the way while they're finishing the custom work on your office.
JERRY. About that: Are bullet-proof windows really necessary?
GOTTSCHALL. Carved bookcases and gold bathroom fixtures aren't necessary, either, but they want you to have them. So leave all that up to the committee and Nellie Winslow; she's decorated two Ritz Carltons and the Mexican ambassador's house. She knows what she's doing. *(Looking at the schedule.)* Tomorrow morning you start with the senior swim club, and you go right on through the week — dedication for the new bowling alley, recovery groups ...
JERRY. *(Reads the list.)* Bucky's Fellowship of Success lunch group —
GOTTSCHALL. Oh, that's a mistake. I offer the blessing there, do it every week.
JERRY. I'll trade you that one for the Women's Weight Loss Ministry Jello Jubilee.
GOTTSCHALL. Just get out there. The people will come to know you. *(Jerry is lost.)* What's on your mind? Too much for the first week?
JERRY. No. No, I'm ready.
GOTTSCHALL. What, then? San Antonio?
JERRY. No. Well, I suppose, of course ... All my time there, years of building and teaching.
GOTTSCHALL. Of course.
JERRY. Promises made ... But, I feel God's called me to do his work here.
GOTTSCHALL. He has. You're famous now.
JERRY. Yes. *(Hugo enters.)*
HUGO. Excuse me, Pastors.
GOTTSCHALL. Where is the girl?
HUGO. On the way. She went to the hospitality center for coffee during the eight-thirty, and she's crowd-surfing her way back here. It's worse than the Christmas light parade out there. *(He stares at the trophy as he listens on the headset.)* Yeah, Dave ... I copy ... Will do ... Fifteen. Out. *(To the pastors.)* On the air in fifteen.

GOTTSCHALL. Get the girl! Let's get this show on the road.
HUGO. Will do, Pastor. *(To Jerry.)* Pastor. *(Hugo exits. Beat.)*
GOTTSCHALL. You are thinking something.
JERRY. Nothing.
GOTTSCHALL. Jerry, I'm your pastor. I don't want you carrying a burden in your heart. Especially not when the ten o'clock is about to start and the TV cameras are looking right at you. I want you out there full of light!
JERRY. I'm fine. I'm excited. So much to think about. *(Beat.)*
GOTTSCHALL. Join me in prayer. *(They pray.)* Lord, your servant, here, loves you. On this, the greatest day in his life of service in your name and the sweet redeeming love of Jesus, he gives praise to you before the world. But, just as the shepherd is happier with the one little sheep from the flock which was lost and found again, Jerry would be more gratified with the praise of one man ... *(Jerry looks up at Gottschall.)* ... than of the thousands, the millions whose eyes will be upon him today. Bring peace to Jerry's heart on this, Lord. In Jesus' name, we pray. Amen.
JERRY. Amen.
GOTTSCHALL. Wherever your daddy is, I do hope he's watching TV at ten o'clock. Now let's get some color on that face!

Scene 2

The pulpit a few minutes later. The orchestra plays as the TV Announcer's voice-over booms over the church orchestra's thrilling prelude.

TV ANNOUNCER (V.O.). From magnificent Rock Baptist Church Houston, RBC Media Ministries brings you Reverend Philip Gottschall's "Mighty Hour of Praise and Glory." With the RBC Symphony Orchestra, the RBC Voices of Jubilee, America's mightiest pipe organ, and Dr. Gottschall's special guests, the legendary Clint Black and Lisa Hartman Black. *(The TV lights inten-*

sify on the pulpit. As the orchestra and organ thunder, and the 300-voice choir triumphantly sings, Gottschall and Jerry take their seats. The song ends, and Gottschall steps to the pulpit.)
GOTTSCHALL. We come to you, Lord, offering all praise and glory to your name. Hallelujah, hallelujah! All praise and glory to our Redeemer, Christ the King. Amen. Amen. My heart overflows with joyfulness this morning as I introduce to you the young man who, after an exhaustive search has been selected to co-pastor with me, to provide for an orderly transition as I ... well, I may appear to be indestructible, but no man is immortal. As you know, I am a firm believer in our doctrine that a congregation selects its pastors. Although I had absolutely no wish whatsoever to interfere in the work of the pastoral search committee, had the decision been mine to make, I would have unequivocally chosen the same servant of God selected by our committee. Please welcome with me a man who is a preacher, a scholar, a professor, an author, a devoted husband and father, one of the true stars in the firmament of our denomination: Dr. Jeremiah Mears. *(Gottschall holds out an arm to welcome Jerry to the pulpit, then steps back and sits. Jerry's hands feel the carving of the pulpit's wood, he gazes at the congregation and savors the moment. He has reached the mountain-top at last. As he opens his mouth to speak, Gottschall rushes up beside him.)* This does not mean I will not be preaching to you anymore. No, no, not at all. Not at *all!* This is not the announcement of my retirement. No, sir. The Lord has kept me sharp and fit, and I will preach his revealed word with every last ounce of life in my body until the day he calls me home! Praise his holy name! *(The orchestra and organ swell as lights fade.)*

Scene 3

Jerry's appearances at activities and meetings on campus.

JERRY. (*At the bowling alley:*) Lord, as we begin this evening in your name, we thank you for the blessing of six new lanes and computerized scoring. We thank you for providing a safe place where families can come together, to have fun, and enjoy ... um ... all-you-can-eat popcorn.

(*At the singles ministry:*) Lord, bless the Christ-centered men and women of this wonderful singles ministry as they come together in your name for a day of fellowship and football. We also ask that you bless our Aggies with victory today as they face off against the Texas Christian University Horned Frogs. Our Aggies ... could use the help.

(*At the High on a Higher Power Alcoholism Recovery Ministry:*)
HUGO. Pastor.
JERRY. You're in this group?
HUGO. I'm in every recovery group on campus.
JERRY. (*Suddenly remembers.*) A woman called my office on Monday, looking for you. Sorry, I forgot to tell you ...
HUGO. A woman?
JERRY. (*Checking pockets.*) Been so busy ... I might have stuffed the message ... said it was personal. She saw your name in the credits on the broadcast, and ... couldn't find your number listed ... (*Finds the message.*) Brenda Lopez.
HUGO. Never heard of her. (*Hugo crumples the message and tosses it aside. Jerry's pager beeps. He checks it and sighs.*)
JERRY. Don't you want to find out what she —
HUGO. Pastor, that woman's either a new problem, or a problem from a time I don't half recall. Either way, I got enough problems just dealing with today.

JERRY. Right. *(The meeting begins.)* Will you all join me in prayer? Lord, bless your servants here who have turned away from drugs and alcohol to get "High on a Higher Power."
HUGO. Amen!

(At the Women's Weight Loss Ministry:)
JERRY. Lord, through prayer, fellowship and vigorous exercise these ladies have shed so many unwanted pounds, and for that we give all praise and thanks to you. *(Quickly checks a "cheat sheet" in his pocket.)* We ask especially for you to give Rowena Martin strength during the hours she's at work; help her to know that every Grand Slam breakfast she serves is not temptation on a plate, but a reminder, a call to be vigilant and trust that faith and fitness will lead her to walk the path you have chosen for her, a more slender Christian.

Scene 4

The Ministers' Room, weeks later; as the final triumphal strains of the closing hymn of the eight-thirty fade, Hugo pours tea for Gottschall, who will preach the televised ten o'clock.

GOTTSCHALL. It's the young people.
HUGO. Yes, sir.
GOTTSCHALL. They're the life blood of a church.
HUGO. We got the biggest youth ministry in the country.
GOTTSCHALL. But it's not getting any bigger. I had hoped a younger co-pastor would bring the youth in.
HUGO. Young people watch TV.
GOTTSCHALL. Out of the question —
HUGO. If he could do the ten o'clock now and then, get some TV exposure —
GOTTSCHALL. You, too?
HUGO. Say, what?
GOTTSCHALL. Bucky Buckholz has been bugging me ... No,

no, it's out of the question. The viewers would cry bloody rebellion if I wasn't in their living rooms every Sunday morning.
HUGO. Just an idea. *(Beat.)* Numbers are up for the eight-thirty, way up.
GOTTSCHALL. Numbers? Look at the numbers that come in envelopes after the broadcast. Look at the numbers on Mastercard and Visa that get called into the prayer partners when I'm on TV. Those are *numbers*. *(Beat.)* Did he tell you to ask me about doing the ten o'clock?
HUGO. Dr. M.? No. I was just thinking on my own.
GOTTSCHALL. Thinking is not in your job description. *(Beat.)* Wire me up. *(Hugo does his audio.)*
HUGO. I'm sorry, Pastor. You know I can't help making dumb comments now and then. Sorry.
GOTTSCHALL. God has a job description for all of us, son. Every now and then we need to be reminded what it is. *(Jerry enters.)*
JERRY. Good morning.
GOTTSCHALL. Morning. It went well, I trust?
JERRY. I must have had over two hundred walk the aisle when I made the call. That's the size of my entire first congregation!
GOTTSCHALL. Praise God. Two hundred!
JERRY. At the eight-thirty.
GOTTSCHALL. Hugo, did we have any spikes at the eight-thirty?
HUGO. No, we stopped spiking a couple weeks ago. Dr. M.'s been doing fine without 'em.
JERRY. You've been spiking the call?
GOTTSCHALL. Just to get things off to a good start, help you make a good name for yourself.
HUGO. It worked real good when you preached that month of guest sermons, before —
JERRY. Why wasn't I told?
GOTTSCHALL. The worship committee makes these decisions.
HUGO. The marketing boys get in on it, too.
JERRY. I should have been told.
GOTTSCHALL. Don't get all huffy. It's not as if we hired actors to do it.
HUGO. No, they're folks that already called in to accept Jesus as

their personal savior.
GOTTSCHALL. They just come to the service instead of being saved on the phone by a prayer partner.
HUGO. They kind of hold it for a day or two. Makes them really want to scoot down that aisle when you make the call.
GOTTSCHALL. It's more meaningful for them to come to Jesus in church.
JERRY. I had no idea ...
GOTTSCHALL. Well, you wouldn't want to make the call and have nobody answer, would you?
JERRY. I want that stopped. Right now.
GOTTSCHALL. It's been stopped.
JERRY. It's dishonest, it's not how God works.
GOTTSCHALL. I know how you feel, Jerry. Dishonesty, secrets, little deceptions — not God's way at all. *(Beat.)* Hugo, could you ...?
HUGO. Yes, sir. *(Hugo removes Jerry's audio.)*
JERRY. Oh, Brenda Lopez left four or five messages for you this week. Please, just call her back so she stops calling me.
HUGO. *(On headset.)* Yeah, Dave ... Got it. Out. *(To Jerry.)* They're waiting on you at the Promise Makers breakfast.
JERRY. Pastor ... *(Jerry checks a printed list and sighs.)* Three breakfasts, lunch, and two prayer coffees ... Pastor, could you and I meet this afternoon, before the spaghetti supper hymn-sing? There are a couple of things we should —
GOTTSCHALL. *(Overlapping.)* No time today, lad. None at all.
JERRY. I've been speaking with Bucky and a few of the deacons about —
GOTTSCHALL. I know all about your secret meetings.
JERRY. They're not secret.
GOTTSCHALL. Was I informed before they occurred?
JERRY. I'm trying to tell you right now.
GOTTSCHALL. Right now, before I preach?
JERRY. Alright, then, this afternoon —
GOTTSCHALL. Bucky's already spoken to me.
JERRY. Oh. About the numbers?
GOTTSCHALL. What about them?
JERRY. Well, we're doing very well at the eight-thirty, but it appears, by analyzing the numbers, that it's at the expense of the

ten o'clock.
GOTTSCHALL. People just want to get a good look at you. Once they're satisfied, they'll go back to sleeping an hour later and coming in for the ten.
JERRY. Bucky thinks I should start doing the ten o'clock. *(Beat.)* At least, some of the time. The majority of deacons feel the same way.
GOTTSCHALL. Oh? There's been a *vote*?
JERRY. No, no. Informal discussions. To be frank, there's great concern about the budget, and that last report from Marketing —
GOTTSCHALL. They don't know Thing One about running a church.
JERRY. They say it's not a matter of message, it's a matter of demographics. *(Hugo listens on his headset.)*
GOTTSCHALL. Look at you: pasty, worn-out, flabby. You got to start taking better care of yourself.
HUGO. *(Overlapping.)* Yeah, Dave ... I copy ... Will do. Out.
JERRY. When can we talk?
HUGO. Pastor? *(Both Jerry and Gottschall look at Hugo.)* Dr. M., I mean. They're still waiting on you.
JERRY. Fine, fine. I'm on the way.
HUGO. *(On headset.)* Hugo to Dave, do you read me? Over.
JERRY. We have to talk. So many things —
GOTTSCHALL. We'll talk. But not now.
HUGO. En route. Five minutes ... I copy. Out.
GOTTSCHALL. Come work out with me tomorrow over at the Houston Club.
JERRY. Why not right here at the Family Life Gym?
GOTTSCHALL. Half of the pledges that built Gottschall College were made in the steam room at the club. If you want to do the ten o'clock — some day — you get some color in your cheeks and you start working the movers and the shakers.
JERRY. Tomorrow's so busy, but —
GOTTSCHALL. You pray on it. If God wants us to talk, he'll give us time to do it. *(Frustrated, Jerry starts to leave.)* Jerry ...
JERRY. Yes?
GOTTSCHALL. Work up a special service for the youth ministry, something they'll want to bring other young people to hear.
HUGO. Only thing kids want to hear about is sex.

GOTTSCHALL. Whatever, just get the young people in the church. It's critical, demographics-wise.
JERRY. I'll do something.
GOTTSCHALL. They like you, but they're not following you.
JERRY. I need to establish more credibility with them, I guess.
GOTTSCHALL. Good, good, lad. I'm pleased with what you're doing here. I am very pleased with you. *(Gottschall has uttered the magic words — and knows it. He flies out of the room.)*

Scene 5

Jerry addresses a Youth Ministry group.

JERRY. I know how you feel. I was a teenager myself. We know how hard it is sometimes to be both a teenager and a Christian at the same time, don't we? My father told me once it's like being a Christmas tree, and every now and then, without any warning whatsoever, your blinker lights start twinkling and flashing. When my father told me that, in the most understanding and sympathetic way, somewhat unfortunately for me, he was speaking in his customary big loud voice, and the boys my age *in the house next door* heard every word. For years after that, every time they saw a light come on in our bathroom window, they'd burst into a chorus of "O, Christmas Tree." *(Beat.)* Beware the flashing colored lights. They're almost always warning lights: traffic hazards, train crossings. Think of the gaudy streets of Las Vegas, millions and millions of flashing colored lights: Whether they're the Devil's lure or God's warning to us, Christians are not seduced by such gaudy displays. Christians resist the temptation. Christians run in the opposite direction, toward a greater light, the light that John wrote about in his gospel: "In him was life, and that life was the light of men ... the true light that gives light to every man." *(Beat.)* When your lights start blinking and flashing, you think about that greater light. And thank God for the precious gift of your life. And you'll know what to do. *(The*

meeting ends. Hugo brings Jerry his jacket and helps him put it on.)
HUGO. Man, I wish I could have heard preaching like that when I was a teenager. Took me twenty years to find the "Off" switch for my blinker lights. *(Jerry puts his jacket on gingerly.)* Pastor, you okay?
JERRY. Just a little stiff from my workout today with Dr. Gottschall.
HUGO. He whooped you.
JERRY. The bicycles, then the rowing machine, then the weights, and the sit-ups and what-have-you. If I did ten, he did twenty. If I did twenty, he did fifty. The man's amazing, he'll live to be a hundred. Praise God. *(Beat.)* He was right about the steam room.
HUGO. Say, what?
JERRY. When they're sitting right next to you stark naked, they're vulnerable. Don't kick 'em when they're down, close 'em!
HUGO. And you closed Dr. G.?
JERRY. Starting week after next, we alternate the ten o'clock.
HUGO. Hallelujah! It's about time … *(Jerry starts to speak, but giggles instead.)* Now that is the first time I have ever, in — what is it now? Nine, ten months? — and I finally see you laughin'.
JERRY. The picture: The co-pastors of the biggest Protestant church in the world, talking in utter seriousness about the future of this church, as we sit in our birthday suits in a room full of steam.
HUGO. That's the picture they should have run in *Time* magazine. *(Jerry gathers his composure.)*
JERRY. Oh, is Accounting's computer system up and running again?
HUGO. Yes, sir, it is.
JERRY. Good. Last week, I didn't get my Sunday numbers until Tuesday.
HUGO. Well, there's a new policy.
JERRY. What new policy?
HUGO. Well, instead of giving me the numbers … now Accounting takes them directly to Pastor's office.
JERRY. No. I don't care where Dr. Gottschall wants his delivered, or when, but I want my copy right away on Sunday.
HUGO. Well, that's not how Mrs. G. wants me to do it.
JERRY. Mrs. G. is not running this church.
HUGO. Now that, right there, is the funniest thing you said today

Scene 6

The Ministers' Room, a month later. The orchestra, choirs and congregation perform the final chorus of the hymn concluding the ten o'clock service. Gottschall looks through Jerry's open briefcase, glancing at documents, rifling through a daily planner, etc.

JERRY. *(Off.)* Not now, page me after the eleven-thirty. *(Gottschall quickly puts things back and starts out of the room, nearly colliding with Jerry.)* Pastor!
GOTTSCHALL. Whoa, there!
JERRY. I didn't realize you were still here. How was your eight-thirty?
GOTTSCHALL. Fine, fine. Good numbers. I told you they'd come back up once the congregation figured out we're alternating the ten o'clock.
JERRY. Numbers are up at every service.
GOTTSCHALL. The flock will follow the shepherd.
JERRY. Some tea?
GOTTSCHALL. No, just leaving.
JERRY. Oh. You weren't waiting for me? To discuss —
GOTTSCHALL. No, just ... just resting my eyes, and I dozed off. Well! Pauline's birthday today. Julia's got a brunch all set up over at River Oaks Country Club. Lee Greenwood's stopping in to sing "Happy Birthday." How about that?
JERRY. I wish I'd known.
GOTTSCHALL. Julia would have invited you, but, of course, you've still got the eleven-thirty to finish.
JERRY. I'll have a gift sent over to Overbrook. *(Takes some papers out of his briefcase, reads.)* We're doing some re-takes at the eleven-thirty, preaching without notes has its pitfalls when you don't have enough time in the week ... *(Jerry senses something out of order in the briefcase.)*
GOTTSCHALL. Well! On my way. Help yourself to some bee

pollen and dried pitted prunes.
JERRY. Pastor?
GOTTSCHALL. Good for the memory. The TV boys never have to stick around for my eleven-thirties.
JERRY. Pastor?
GOTTSCHALL. Yes.
JERRY. About my memo ...
GOTTSCHALL. I've seen no memorandum. Must run now.
JERRY. Mrs. Neville —
GOTTSCHALL. Yes.
JERRY. She's had my parking spot labeled "Co-Pastor."
GOTTSCHALL. Of course.
JERRY. But yours still says "Pastor."
GOTTSCHALL. I don't have time for —
JERRY. In my memo ... Either both spots should be labeled "Co-Pastor," or —
GOTTSCHALL. Trivialities, lad. Inconsequential trivialities that have nothing whatsoever to do with God's work. You learn your lines, now, get your message down pat for the TV cameras. *(Gottschall flies out of the room.)*
JERRY. Dr. Gottschall ...
GOTTSCHALL. *(Off.)* Bee pollen, lad. Bee pollen and dried pitted prunes.

Scene 7

Just before a meeting of the High on a Higher Power Recovery Ministry. Hugo is twitchier than usual. Jerry comes up to him and speaks so no one else can hear.

JERRY. We've got a few minutes before the rest of the group gets here.
HUGO. Recovery meetings don't need any of this mystery, thank you very much.

JERRY. I'm sorry about that, but it's serious, Hugo. Very serious.
HUGO. That woman?
JERRY. Brenda Lopez. She came to my office today.
HUGO. I don't know her.
JERRY. I canceled a meeting with the Christmas electrical parade committee, even though that's already thirty thousand over budget. I had to spend time with Brenda, once she told me —
HUGO. *(Jumps.)* Whatever she's claiming, don't —
JERRY. Hugo, she does know you. Or did.
HUGO. How do you know?
JERRY. You knew her very well when you were in Albuquerque.
HUGO. No, don't think so.
JERRY. She knows you've got "Jesus Wept" tattooed on the right side of your rear end.
HUGO. Albuquerque …
JERRY. Twelve, thirteen years ago?
HUGO. Yeah, maybe.
JERRY. Hugo, you're a father.
HUGO. No.
JERRY. You and Brenda have a son.
HUGO. I don't remember any woman in Albuquerque! I don't half-remember Albuquerque! All due respect, but please, just butt right out of my business, and quit believing every lie any stray dog tells you.
JERRY. I believe Brenda. She's in Houston now. She's a Christian. I prayed with her today.
HUGO. I'm not seeing her.
JERRY. The boy needs his father.
HUGO. Yeah, well, I needed a father once.
JERRY. Don't do to him what your father did to you. A fatherless boy feels like he doesn't really exist in this world. You know that.
HUGO. You don't know —
JERRY. You felt so worthless you nearly killed yourself. Do you want that to happen to this boy someday? He's your son. It's your job to be his father.
HUGO. I'm sick of everybody telling me what my job is! *(Jerry waits.)* Is she still fat?
JERRY. So you do remember.

HUGO. There was a fat girl in Albuquerque I recall somewhat.
JERRY. She was a prostitute. She told me. And she sold drugs.
HUGO. We weren't country club material. Okay, say she's got a kid, and she got pregnant around the time I was in Albuquerque, that does not prove that I'm the kid's father.
JERRY. Hugo, I know how you feel. I know you're scared.
HUGO. Tell her you couldn't find me. *(Hugo tears off, but Jerry is quick, and stops him. Hugo struggles in Jerry's grip.)*
JERRY. This kid's in trouble. He needs a father. He needs a role model.
HUGO. Role model?
JERRY. Yes.
HUGO. I'm a role model for a car wreck.
JERRY. Twelve years old, that's all he is. And he sneaks out, gets drunk ... burglary, arson. He idolizes the neighborhood crack dealer.
HUGO. Well, the apple don't fall very far from the big, fat tree.
JERRY. You can save this boy. You can be responsible for him. But if you reject him, you're handing him a death sentence. You and I know, it'll just be a matter of time. And you don't have the right to do that. Do you hear me? Only God had the right to sacrifice his son, and he did it so that we may have eternal life, our sins washed away by the blood, the suffering of Jesus. You accepted Jesus as your savior. You turned your life over to him. He brought you here. And now he's brought your son to you. You reject this boy, that's ... that's rejecting Jesus. *(Hugo stops struggling.)* Your son ... he has a name.
HUGO. Don't say it!
JERRY. Vincent. Your son's name is Vincent. *(Hugo sobs, a defensive little boy.)*
HUGO. You're just doing this 'cause you're still mad at your daddy for walking out on you.
JERRY. He didn't walk out.
HUGO. Your daddy ... he could look you in the eye and know what you're thinking, feel how you're hurting. Make you feel safe. I can't be that.
JERRY. You can be more than he ever was.
HUGO. He saved me.
JERRY. No, God saved you. You saved yourself. But Dad ... Dad

wasn't God. He loved God, but he was a closer. He didn't know where the selling stopped and the saving began. He looked you in the eye because that's what salesmen do. Good eye contact establishes control. Then he told you, "I know how you feel." He was establishing credibility, see? Then he uncovered your needs, didn't he? "You feel lost, son, don't you? Sure you do. Your life is like being in the passenger seat of a car doing eighty miles an hour, and nobody's at the wheel, isn't that right? A dead man for sure. I *know* how you feel." Then he'd go on to the features of his product. "Son, you have eternal life with Jesus, do you know that? Eternal life!" Then the benefits, "You'll wake up every morning, knowing that somebody's there for you, looking out for you; somebody with a plan for your life." Need, feature, benefit. Then, the close, "Will you pray with me now? I'll be right here with you. I'm Christ's rabid dog, and I won't let you go. Pray with me." Sound familiar, Hugo?
HUGO. You're jealous of him!
JERRY. You can be there for your son. My father couldn't do that.
HUGO. No matter how hard you try, no matter what heights you climb, you can never be bigger than your old man, can you?
JERRY. I know how you feel. Hugo, I do. But this isn't about me. Or you. It's about a twelve-year old boy named Vincent. You're responsible for this boy.
HUGO. I do such a piss-poor job of being responsible for me, how can I — ?
JERRY. I'll help you. We'll get him enrolled here at Rock, get him away from the criminal element.
HUGO. Have you seen him?
JERRY. No.
HUGO. Oh. I was just wondering if he ...
JERRY. Brenda wants me to call her tonight. She's bringing him to the ten o'clock tomorrow morning.
HUGO. Oh, Lord. Oh, Lord! *(Beat.)* What if he don't want to see me?
JERRY. Hugo, believe me, he wants to see you.
HUGO. Be with me. You doing the ten tomorrow?
JERRY. Yes. I'll be right there with you.
HUGO. One thing, Pastor.
JERRY. Yes?

HUGO. Don't say anything to Dr. G. about this.
JERRY. Why? He wouldn't —
HUGO. I know him better than you. You and God may be okay with bringing Brenda here, and my ... my son. But I don't know how okay I am with all of this yet. So, if it's all the same to you, I'd like to be the one to tell Dr. G., you know, once I get used to it all.
JERRY. Fine. I won't say a word.
HUGO. So ... tomorrow after the ten o'clock? *(Beat.)* Okay. All right. Well ... Pastor, you got a room full of recovering Christian alcoholics in there who could really use a prayer from you right now to get the meeting going. Don't mind me if tonight I just sort of hang out behind the back row. I'm feeling a little shaky. *(Jerry moves to where the meeting is starting and leads a prayer.)*
JERRY. Heavenly Father, we come before you tonight, your children, with full faith in you and your presence in our lives.

Scene 8

The Ministers' Room, that Sunday, following the eight-thirty service. It is the last Sunday of Advent.

GOTTSCHALL. *(Enters quickly as the final music of the organ postlude ("O Come, O Come, Emmanuel") fades. He pours a cup of tea and grabs a bag of dried pitted prunes, devouring them as he gathers his things to leave. He checks his watch — getting late! — fumbles with his microphone and finally hollers in exasperation.)* Hugo! Where in Creation are you?
HUGO. *(Off.)* Coming!
GOTTSCHALL. I got meetings to get to! *(Hugo flies into the room, wearing a new jacket and tie, nervously touching his freshly combed hair.)*
HUGO. Sorry, Pastor. I was in the men's room.
GOTTSCHALL. What are you all slicked up for? *(Hugo removes*

Gottschall's microphone pack.)
HUGO. Um ... Nothing special. I try to look presentable for the ten o'clock. In case the TV cameras pick me up in the background, or something.
GOTTSCHALL. All slicked up for Dr. Mears' ten o'clock.
HUGO. I'm gonna slick myself up for all the ten o'clocks now. New policy.
GOTTSCHALL. Lots of new policies around here.
HUGO. Yes, sir! You can feel the old excitement coming back to Rock, can't you?
GOTTSCHALL. I'll tell you what I feel, Hugo. And I'm telling you this because I know, and Mrs. Gottschall knows, every word you hear goes right back to Dr. Mears and his cronies. *(Hugo stunned, stammers, unable to answer.)* Sides are being taken, and I will not have it. I will not have dissension. I am still pastor of this church, do you hear me? Whisperings, secret meetings, secret plans. Every day a new program, new policy, new major expenditures about which I was not informed — not even consulted! Memoranda, mountains of memoranda, yes! All of it after the deeds are done!
HUGO. But, you're Pastor, you should be —
GOTTSCHALL. Don't deny your role in this ... this conspiracy.
HUGO. Say, what?
GOTTSCHALL. "A false witness will not go unpunished, and he who pours out lies will not go free."
HUGO. Pastor, do you think I'm lying to you? I'm not. I swear!
GOTTSCHALL. Don't swear to me. That's between you and God, son. You and God.
HUGO. Pastor, you know I'm completely devoted to you. I'll do anything you ask.
GOTTSCHALL. What's most heartbreaking is that Mrs. Gottschall no longer feels she can trust you. She needs to know what's happening on campus. I cannot be everywhere at once, and we've relied upon you. As Paul relied upon Silas!
HUGO. I'm still her eyes and ears everywhere! I tell her everything!
GOTTSCHALL. Everything?
HUGO. Everything!
GOTTSCHALL. Did you tell her about your meeting last night

with Dr. Mears?
HUGO. What meeting?
GOTTSCHALL. Hugo. "Devise not evil against thy neighbour."
HUGO. Last night? Dr. M. gave the blessing at High on a Higher Power.
GOTTSCHALL. You're denying then, that you and he met privately before the meeting?
HUGO. We just said, you know, what's new and what-have-you.
GOTTSCHALL. You're denying he was attempting to recruit you for — ?
HUGO. We just said *hello*.
GOTTSCHALL. I was told the two of you were —
HUGO. Told by who? What is going on around here?
GOTTSCHALL. I will not have plots and secrets. I will not! We are here to serve God, glorify his holy name and bring souls to Jesus. There is no place here for plotting, and whispering, and secrets!
HUGO. All right! Okay, about that meeting: I hope you won't think too much less of me for what I'm going to tell you, but it has to do with something stupid I did I ain't proud of. *(Hugo summons the courage to reveal his parenthood to Gottschall, but before he can speak, Jerry enters and senses the tension in the room.)*
JERRY. Good morning. Pastor. Hugo.
GOTTSCHALL. Good morning.
JERRY. The eight-thirty…?
GOTTSCHALL. Record numbers for the last eight-thirty before Christmas. Record numbers, lad!
JERRY. *(Attempting humor.)* Well, I hope a few thousand are left to show up for my ten o'clock. *(Beat.)*
GOTTSCHALL. I'm due at a meeting. Hugo, you give Mrs. Gottschall a call and give her a complete report right now on what we were just discussing. Will you do that?
HUGO. Yes, sir, I will.
GOTTSCHALL. Jerry, I'll see you tonight for the Christmas electric light parade.
JERRY. Yes.
HUGO. I'll take you two up to the Pastor's float at six-fifteen.
GOTTSCHALL. Don't forget to make that call, Hugo. God bless you, lads. *(Gottschall exits.)*

JERRY. Did you just tell him?
HUGO. No. That was nothing. Are they here?
JERRY. I put Brenda and Vincent in the second pew, center aisle, left side.
HUGO. Lord, get me through this morning.
JERRY. I assigned an usher to bring them back here after the service. *(The organ and bell choir prelude to the ten o'cock service begins, "O, Little Town of Bethlehem," played with sensitivity and grace. Hugo leans in to Jerry.)*
HUGO. Does he ... *(Almost a whisper.)* The kid, does he ...
JERRY. Yes, quite a bit. Especially the eyes. The resemblance is remarkable.
HUGO. Oh, Lord.
JERRY. Fidgety. He's got a tattoo, but at least it says, "Mother."
HUGO. *(Deep breath.)* Did Brenda say if she wants to — Oh, Lord ... *(Gottschall returns, pausing at the door as he sees Jerry and Hugo deep in intense conversation. At first they don't see him.)*
JERRY. *(To Hugo.)* It's all right, go ahead and ask.
GOTTSCHALL. I hope I'm not interrupting something private.
JERRY. No.
HUGO. No, nothing.
GOTTSCHALL. What are you two whispering about?
JERRY. We were ... Frankly, Pastor, I've been counseling Hugo about a ... a situation, a burden he's been struggling with.
GOTTSCHALL. Hugo, I'm your pastor. If your heart's burdened, you come to me, unless you'd rather —
HUGO. No! I mean, I would, but this particular burden came to Dr. M., and he brought it to me, and —
GOTTSCHALL. *(Retrieves his bag of prunes.)* I'll leave you two alone now to get your story straight.
JERRY. Pastor —
HUGO. It's not what you think. *(Gottschall waves them off and leaves in a fury. Hugo listens on his headset.)* Yeah, Dave ... I copy. Two minutes. Out. *(To Jerry.)* I got to do your audio.

Scene 9

The organ and bell choir hymn from the last scene becomes a digital, almost carnival-like, "electronic music" version of "O, Little Town of Bethlehem" for the Christmas electrical parade.

The Ministers' Room, six-fifteen that evening. Gottschall waits, dressed in a suit. Jerry enters, wearing a long overcoat, gloves and wool scarf. The parade music repeats in the distance.

GOTTSCHALL. Well, lad ... The parade just goes down Post Oak Boulevard, not all the way up to the Yukon Territory.
JERRY. Aren't you wearing an overcoat?
GOTTSCHALL. Not at all, lad. Not at all.
JERRY. It's pretty bitter out there.
GOTTSCHALL. Never had so much as a head cold since the day I took the pulpit. I'm not so easy to knock down. No, lad. It's not bitter *outside*. *(Beat.)*
JERRY. Shouldn't Hugo be here by now?
GOTTSCHALL. No, Hugo should not.
JERRY. Yes. He's supposed to take us up to the Pastor's float.
GOTTSCHALL. Hugo Taney is no longer an employee of this church.
JERRY. What?
GOTTSCHALL. His employment, regretfully, had to be terminated.
JERRY. When? On what grounds? What the — Who — ?
GOTTSCHALL. His employment was terminated by the operations manager this afternoon.
JERRY. I was here all afternoon. Why wasn't I consulted?
GOTTSCHALL. Insubordination. We cannot tolerate insubordinate —
JERRY. You did this! This was you —
GOTTSCHALL. Collusion, plotting, working against the best

interests of this church ... We cannot have it.
JERRY. What collusion?
GOTTSCHALL. How you've changed since you came to Rock. I should have seen it coming, but I trusted you. But that's my nature, to be trusting.
JERRY. What did you do to Hugo?
GOTTSCHALL. I pray for you, Jerry. Julia and I both pray for you. We pray that this unbridled lust for power by which Satan's attempting to corrupt your soul —
JERRY. What did you do to Hugo?
GOTTSCHALL. He had to be let go. His behavior was destructive to the best interests of the church.
JERRY. That's not good enough.
GOTTSCHALL. I'm not surprised losing your little spy's made you go off the deep end.
JERRY. You're delusional.
GOTTSCHALL. Son, I'm sharp as a chisel. And I'm not the only one who's seen you two, whispering, making secret plans, plotting to render me irrelevant to my own church. *(Jerry starts to leave.)* Where are you going?
JERRY. I've got to find him.
GOTTSCHALL. You've got to lead this parade, young pup! You're on the Pastor's float! This is history! The first time since they started this thing anyone's up on the Pastor's float beside me! There are over two hundred thousand people out there waiting to view this historic moment, stuffing their faces with popcorn. And snow cones. Every TV station in Texas has a camera crew shivering out there, waiting for you. *(Beat. Jerry doesn't leave.)*
JERRY. He loves you. He'd have done anything for you, anything.
GOTTSCHALL. At one time, yes, that was true. Before his loyalty was corrupted.
JERRY. His loyalty — my loyalty to you, for that matter — has never been corrupted.
GOTTSCHALL. "These six things doth the Lord hate:
JERRY. *(Talking over Gottschall.)* He's lost without this church. He can't handle his life without this church! And you drove him from it!
GOTTSCHALL. *(Continuing over Jerry.)* "A proud look, a lying tongue, and hands that shed innocent blood, an heart that

deviseth wicked imaginations,
JERRY. He won't survive. You've sacrificed him to your own glory, your vanity!
GOTTSCHALL. *(Thundering. The final words.)* "Feet that be swift in running to mischief, a false witness that speaketh lies, and he that soweth discord among brethren."
JERRY. You've sacrificed Hugo. Sacrificed him, and his son. *(Beat.)*
GOTTSCHALL. Hugo has no son.
JERRY. Yes, he does. He met him for the first time this morning, right after the ten o'clock. *(Jerry lets this sink in.)* The mother saw Hugo's name in the credits on the broadcast, my first Sunday here. The day you presented me as your co-pastor. She called me, and I was able to bring them together.
GOTTSCHALL. She called *you*?
JERRY. Yes.
GOTTSCHALL. She called the *co-pastor*.
JERRY. Hugo was afraid you'd think less of him for having fathered, and abandoned, a son. He didn't know there was a child, by the way, until last night. I told him, in private, just before High on a Higher Power started. *(Beat.)* He so wanted you to be proud of him, to be pleased with him.
GOTTSCHALL. He shouldn't have been afraid.
JERRY. That sorry, abused, wretched, little soul was clinging to your mighty rock for life itself.
GOTTSCHALL. He would have shared this burden with me if you hadn't poisoned him with your whisperings.
JERRY. Your approval was his life. Your rejection will likely be his death.
GOTTSCHALL. Well, then, go find him. Go look in every beer bar and dope den in Houston. I'll do the parade. The TV boys can get their historic two-pastors-on-the-float pictures next year.
JERRY. Next year?
GOTTSCHALL. The parade's an annual event.
JERRY. Pastor ... Pastor, God brought me here to lead this church.
GOTTSCHALL. I brought you here, and God's been making me pay dearly for it ever since.
JERRY. You have got to allow God's plan to unfold.

GOTTSCHALL. How do you know what God's plan is? He's told you? I thought he hasn't spoken to you in a long time. We've all heard you whine about that often enough.
JERRY. He led me here. You know that.
GOTTSCHALL. If he led you here it was to test me, to prove that I am still completely capable of pastoring this church without the so-called assistance of —
JERRY. *(Overlapping.)* You promised me that after a brief transitional period, you would retire.
GOTTSCHALL. I recall no such promise. I said we'd see what God does. In God's time.
JERRY. Are you waiting for God to strike you dead? Step aside now, enjoy your retirement —
GOTTSCHALL. *Step aside?* I'm stepping up on to the Pastor's float. I gotta go holler, "Happy Birthday, Jesus!" Amen!

Scene 10

On the Pastor's Float in the Christmas electrical parade. The digital "O Little Town of Bethlehem" continues, louder and more annoyingly. Jerry and Gottschall wave to the cheering crowd, a blinding array of twinkling colored lights reflects on their frozen smiles.

JERRY. This is the first thing that's going to go. This carnival.
GOTTSCHALL. Membership recruitment, lad. People want to be part of the excitement.
JERRY. Big numbers.
GOTTSCHALL. Big numbers make big deeds possible. God's work.
JERRY. Where is God in all this?
GOTTSCHALL. God is in every face in that crowd. Look at that! Praise Jesus! Happy Birthday, Jesus!
JERRY. Is this what Jesus envisioned when he told Peter he would

build his church upon a rock? A church built on a dinner theater and two swimming pools?
GOTTSCHALL. You have no vision, you have no sense of the greatness of God.
JERRY. The greatness of Dr. Philip J. Gottschall ...
GOTTSCHALL. I thought you had what it would take to lead this church someday.
JERRY. What this church needs is to be a church, not Las Vegas.
GOTTSCHALL. What's happened to you?
JERRY. The church is not the rock. You're not the rock, I'm not the rock. Jesus is the rock.
GOTTSCHALL. You, who were so eager to work with us —
JERRY. I was eager — I *am* eager — to do God's work. Not to bless bowling alleys and ride in parades.
GOTTSCHALL. You came here for the same reason you do anything: to holler, "Hey, Daddy! Look at me!" *(Shouts.)* Happy Birthday, Jesus! Praise his holy name!
JERRY. Then why did you hire me in the first place? To be the son you never had? So you could keep up with the rest of the big-timers, putting their sons in their pulpits? That's not succession or continuity; it's immortality.
GOTTSCHALL. *(Shouting.)* Happy Birthday, Jesus!
JERRY. You never wanted a successor. You wanted me to be your son. Your obedient son.
GOTTSCHALL. No, lad. That's not what I wanted. That's what *you* wanted. *(Beat.)*
JERRY. You're never going to let me lead this church, are you?
GOTTSCHALL. It's in God's hands.
JERRY. You haven't answered my question. Are you ever going to —
GOTTSCHALL. You're a whiner, lad. Whining, whining about hearing God's voice. Why in Creation would God want to talk to a whiner?
JERRY. And God speaks to you?
GOTTSCHALL. Every day, son. Every day. *(The music and cheering grow louder.)*
JERRY. *(Shouting.)* How can you hear him over all this noise?
GOTTSCHALL. *(Shouting.)* Happy Birthday, Jesus! *(To Jerry.)* TV cameras. Big smile! *(The music and cheering are deafening. The*

lights flash faster. Gottschall waves and smiles. Jerry, like a wild animal seconds before it becomes road-kill, freezes, then leaps off the float, and all is darkness.)

Scene 11

The persistent, shrill digital music of the Christmas electric light parade becomes a solitary electronic keyboard playing the old hymn, "Faith of Our Fathers."

A rural swap meet, Sunday, several months later, about an hour before the doors open to the public. Jerry, in shirtsleeves, gazes outward. Hugo joins him.

HUGO. Pastor?
JERRY. Are we all set?
HUGO. Yeah, we got a good crowd today. A lot more dealers came in to do their set-up early so they could join in. Oh, and Loretta Fink remembered to bring her grandson's keyboard in to play the hymns on. We're big-time religion now.
JERRY. Sounds fine.
HUGO. One of the churches in town sent over some hymn books for us. The preacher saw the story in *Time* magazine.
JERRY. Good.
HUGO. Vincent and your boys got the tables all pushed back at the barbecue stand, and the crowd's waiting, so if you want to get started ...
JERRY. Thank you. *(But Jerry doesn't move.)*
HUGO. We only got an hour before the swap meet doors open to the public. Pastor?
JERRY. Sorry. I was just ... listening. *(Hugo leaves Jerry alone. Jerry continues to listen. The electronic keyboard "Faith of Our Fathers" is drowned out by the Rock orchestra and choir concluding the same hymn as lights come up on Gottschall at the Rock pulpit.)*

GOTTSCHALL. In these last few months, my beloved Julia and I have prayed every day for Dr. Mears. We don't know why he left so suddenly. I'm sure he believes he was called. *Time* magazine seems to think it's an obscene waste of talent for him to be selling vitamins at a swap meet somewhere way out in the country. But I know his daddy was a salesman who served God in his own way, and I suspect ... Well, like father, like son, as they say ... in his image. *(Beat.)* This morning, we pray on Paul's message from Corinth to the emerging church in Rome. He wrote: "We know that all things work together for good to them that love God, to them who are *called* ... " *(Beat.)* And about Dr. Jeremiah Mears, I shall say no more. Except to say, God be with him. *(Lights fade, except for a warm pool of light on Jerry.)*

JERRY. Elijah, hiding in the cave, heard God's whisper. God promised Elijah he would reveal himself to him. And though wind swept through the desert, fire raged and earthquake thundered, God was not in them. God came, God spoke, to Elijah in a *whisper*. *(Beat. Jerry speaks in a big voice now, his father's voice.)* It is possible that God was revealing himself to Elijah the whole time. But how could Elijah hear God's whisper over the deafening sound of the wind, and the fire and the earthquake? *(Quietly.)* How could God's whisper be heard? *(Beat.)* Jesus said: "What I tell you in the dark, speak in the daylight; what is whispered in your ear, proclaim from the roofs." Proclaim! Shout! BIG voice! "What is whispered in your ear ... " What God whispers in your ear. *(Beat.)* Lord, I pray ... I pray ... I pray to you, let me hear your sweet voice, your whisper. I will proclaim. I will shout! I will proclaim your love, and your salvation, and your gospel. I have never in my life felt closer to you, my father, my father in Heaven, than I do right now. Right here. In this quiet place. Whisper in my ear, and I will proclaim. I will. *(Quietly.)* Lord? Lord, I'm listening. I'm listening. *(Beat. Jerry suddenly looks Heavenward. He whispers:)* Amen. *(Lights fade.)*

End of Play

PROPERTY LIST

Briefcase (JERRY)
Headset (HUGO)
Clip-on microphones/transmitters to put on Gottschall and Jerry (HUGO)
Tea tray with boxes of tea, teapot, 2 cups, 2 saucers, spoons, sugar bowl, creamer (HUGO)
Tea kettle (HUGO)
Sermon notes (JERRY)
Bible (JERRY, GOTTSCHALL)
Computer printouts — "the numbers" (HUGO)
Ping-pong trophy, in wrapped gift box (HUGO)
Greeting card with trophy box (HUGO)
Bag of prunes (GOTTSCHALL)
Typed schedule of events (GOTTSCHALL)
Pager (JERRY)
"Cheat sheet" index card (JERRY)
Daily planner — in briefcase (JERRY)
Files and papers — in briefcase (JERRY)
Scarf, gloves, overcoat (JERRY)

SOUND EFFECTS

300-voice choir, congregation, orchestra and organ hymn
Orchestra plays, as TV voice-over announcer speaks
Orchestra and organ swell
Triumphal hymn fade-out
Orchestra, choirs and congregation sing final verse of hymn
Organ postlude, "O Come, O Come, Emmanuel"
Organ prelude, "O Little Town of Bethlehem"
Electronic keyboard and bell choir, "O Little Town of Bethlehem"
Electric keyboard, "Faith of Our Fathers"
Parade crowd cheering
Orchestra and choir, "Faith of Our Fathers"

NEW PLAYS

★ **HONOUR by Joanna Murray-Smith.** In a series of intense confrontations, a wife, husband, lover and daughter negotiate the forces of passion, history, responsibility and honour. "HONOUR makes for surprisingly interesting viewing. Tight, crackling dialogue (usually played out in punchy verbal duels) captures characters unable to deal with emotions ... Murray-Smith effectively places her characters in situations that strip away pretense." –*Variety* "... the play's virtues are strong: a distinctive theatrical voice, passionate concerns ... HONOUR might just capture a few honors of its own." –*Time Out Magazine* [1M, 3W] ISBN: 0-8222-1683-3

★ **MR. PETERS' CONNECTIONS by Arthur Miller.** Mr. Miller describes the protagonist as existing in a dream-like state when the mind is "freed to roam from real memories to conjectures, from trivialities to tragic insights, from terror of death to glorying in one's being alive." With this memory play, the Tony Award and Pulitzer Prize-winner reaffirms his stature as the world's foremost dramatist. "... a cross between Joycean stream-of-consciousness and Strindberg's dream plays, sweetened with a dose of William Saroyan's philosophical whimsy ... CONNECTIONS is most intriguing ..." –*The NY Times* [5M, 3W] ISBN: 0-8222-1687-6

★ **THE WAITING ROOM by Lisa Loomer.** Three women from different centuries meet in a doctor's waiting room in this dark comedy about the timeless quest for beauty – and its cost. "... THE WAITING ROOM ... is a bold, risky melange of conflicting elements that is ... terrifically moving ... There's no resisting the fierce emotional pull of the play." –*The NY Times* "... one of the high points of this year's Off-Broadway season ... THE WAITING ROOM is well worth a visit." –*Back Stage* [7M, 4W, flexible casting] ISBN: 0-8222-1594-2

★ **THE OLD SETTLER by John Henry Redwood.** A sweet-natured comedy about two church-going sisters in 1943 Harlem and the handsome young man who rents a room in their apartment. "For all of its decent sentiments, THE OLD SETTLER avoids sentimentality. It has the authenticity and lack of pretense of an Early American sampler." –*The NY Times* "We've had some fine plays Off-Broadway this season, and this is one of the best." –*The NY Post* [1M, 3W] ISBN: 0-8-222-1642-6

★ **LAST TRAIN TO NIBROC by Arlene Hutton.** In 1940 two young strangers share a seat on a train bound east only to find their paths will cross again. "All aboard. LAST TRAIN TO NIBROC is a sweetly told little chamber romance." –*Show Business* "... [a] gently charming little play, reminiscent of Thornton Wilder in its look at rustic Americans who are to be treasured for their simplicity and directness ..." –*Associated Press* "The old formula of boy wins girls, boy loses girl, boy wins girl still works ... [a] well-made play that perfectly captures a slice of small-town-life-gone-by." –*Back Stage* [1M, 1W] ISBN: 0-8222-1753-8

★ **OVER THE RIVER AND THROUGH THE WOODS by Joe DiPietro.** Nick sees both sets of his grandparents every Sunday for dinner. This is routine until he has to tell them that he's been offered a dream job in Seattle. The news doesn't sit so well. "A hilarious family comedy that is even funnier than his long running musical revue *I Love You, You're Perfect, Now Change*." –*Back Stage* "Loaded with laughs every step of the way." –*Star-Ledger* [3M, 3W] ISBN: 0-8222-1712-0

★ **SIDE MAN by Warren Leight.** 1999 Tony Award winner. This is the story of a broken family and the decline of jazz as popular entertainment. "... a tender, deeply personal memory play about the turmoil in the family of a jazz musician as his career crumbles at the dawn of the age of rock-and-roll ..." –*The NY Times* "[SIDE MAN] is an elegy for two things – a lost world and a lost love. When the two notes sound together in harmony, it is moving and graceful ..." –*The NY Daily News* "An atmospheric memory play ... with crisp dialogue and clearly drawn characters ... reflects the passing of an era with persuasive insight ... The joy and despair of the musicians is skillfully illustrated." –*Variety* [5M, 3W] ISBN: 0-8222-1721-X

DRAMATISTS PLAY SERVICE, INC.
440 Park Avenue South, New York, NY 10016   212-683-8960   Fax 212-213-1539
postmaster@dramatists.com   www.dramatists.com

NEW PLAYS

★ **CLOSER by Patrick Marber.** Winner of the 1998 Olivier Award for Best Play and the 1999 New York Drama Critics Circle Award for Best Foreign Play. Four lives intertwine over the course of four and a half years in this densely plotted, stinging look at modern love and betrayal. "CLOSER is a sad, savvy, often funny play that casts a steely, unblinking gaze at the world of relationships and lets you come to your own conclusions ... CLOSER does not merely hold your attention; it burrows into you." –*New York Magazine* "A powerful, darkly funny play about the cosmic collision between the sun of love and the comet of desire." –*Newsweek Magazine* [2M, 2W] ISBN: 0-8222-1722-8

★ **THE MOST FABULOUS STORY EVER TOLD by Paul Rudnick.** A stage manager, headset and prompt book at hand, brings the house lights to half, then dark, and cues the creation of the world. Throughout the play, she's in control of everything. In other words, she's either God, or she thinks she is. "Line by line, Mr. Rudnick may be the funniest writer for the stage in the United States today ... One-liners, epigrams, withering put-downs and flashing repartee: These are the candles that Mr. Rudnick lights instead of cursing the darkness ... a testament to the virtues of laughing ... and in laughter, there is something like the memory of Eden." –*The NY Times* "Funny it is ... consistently, rapaciously, deliriously ... easily the funniest play in town." –*Variety* [4M, 5W] ISBN: 0-8222-1720-1

★ **A DOLL'S HOUSE by Henrik Ibsen, adapted by Frank McGuinness.** Winner of the 1997 Tony Award for Best Revival. "New, raw, gut-twisting and gripping. Easily the hottest drama this season." –*USA Today* "Bold, brilliant and alive." –*The Wall Street Journal* "A thunderclap of an evening that takes your breath away." –*Time Magazine* [4M, 4W, 2 boys] ISBN: 0-8222-1636-1

★ **THE HERBAL BED by Peter Whelan.** The play is based on actual events which occurred in Stratford-upon-Avon in the summer of 1613, when William Shakespeare's elder daughter was publicly accused of having a sexual liaison with a married neighbor and family friend. "In his probing new play, THE HERBAL BED ... Peter Whelan muses about a sidelong event in the life of Shakespeare's family and creates a finely textured tapestry of love and lies in the early 17th-century Stratford." –*The NY Times* "It is a first rate drama with interesting moral issues of truth and expediency." –*The NY Post* [5M, 3W] ISBN: 0-8222-1675-2

★ **SNAKEBIT by David Marshall Grant.** A study of modern friendship when put to the test. "... a rather smart and absorbing evening of water-cooler theater, the intimate sort of Off-Broadway experience that has you picking apart the recognizable characters long after the curtain calls." –*The NY Times* "Off-Broadway keeps on presenting us with compelling reasons for going to the theater. The latest is SNAKEBIT, David Marshall Grant's smart new comic drama about being thirtysomething and losing one's way in life." –*The NY Daily News* [3M, 1W] ISBN: 0-8222-1724-4

★ **A QUESTION OF MERCY by David Rabe.** The Obie Award-winning playwright probes the sensitive and controversial issue of doctor-assisted suicide in the age of AIDS in this poignant drama. "There are devastating ironies in Mr. Rabe's beautifully considered, piercingly clear-eyed work ..." –*The NY Times* "With unsettling candor and disturbing insight, the play arouses pity and understanding of a troubling subject ... Rabe's provocative tale is an affirmation of dignity that rings clear and true." –*Variety* [6M, 1W] ISBN: 0-8222-1643-4

★ **DIMLY PERCEIVED THREATS TO THE SYSTEM by Jon Klein.** Reality and fantasy overlap with hilarious results as this unforgettable family attempts to survive the nineties. "Here's a play whose point about fractured families goes to the heart, mind – and ears." –*The Washington Post* "... an end-of-the millennium comedy about a family on the verge of a nervous breakdown ... Trenchant and hilarious ..." –*The Baltimore Sun* [2M, 4W] ISBN: 0-8222-1677-9

DRAMATISTS PLAY SERVICE, INC.
440 Park Avenue South, New York, NY 10016 212-683-8960 Fax 212-213-1539
postmaster@dramatists.com   www.dramatists.com

NEW PLAYS

★ **AS BEES IN HONEY DROWN by Douglas Carter Beane.** Winner of the John Gassner Playwriting Award. A hot young novelist finds the subject of his new screenplay in a New York socialite who leads him into the world of *Auntie Mame* and *Breakfast at Tiffany's*, before she takes him for a ride. "A delicious soufflé of a satire ... [an] extremely entertaining fable for an age that always chooses image over substance." –*The NY Times* "... A witty assessment of one of the most active and relentless industries in a consumer society ... the creation of 'hot' young things, which the media have learned to mass produce with efficiency and zeal." –*The NY Daily News* [3M, 3W, flexible casting] ISBN: 0-8222-1651-5

★ **STUPID KIDS by John C. Russell.** In rapid, highly stylized scenes, the story follows four high-school students as they make their way from first through eighth period and beyond, struggling with the fears, frustrations, and longings peculiar to youth. "In STUPID KIDS ... playwright John C. Russell gets the opera of adolescence to a T ... The stylized teenspeak of STUPID KIDS ... suggests that Mr. Russell may have hidden a tape recorder under a desk in study hall somewhere and then scoured the tapes for good quotations ... it is the kids' insular, ceaselessly churning world, a pre-adult world of Doritos and libidos, that the playwright seeks to lay bare." –*The NY Times* "STUPID KIDS [is] a sharp-edged ... whoosh of teen angst and conformity anguish. It is also very funny." –*NY Newsday* [2M, 2W] ISBN: 0-8222-1698-1

★ **COLLECTED STORIES by Donald Margulies.** From Obie Award-winner Donald Margulies comes a provocative analysis of a student-teacher relationship that turns sour when the protégé becomes a rival. "With his fine ear for detail, Margulies creates an authentic, insular world, and he gives equal weight to the opposing viewpoints of two formidable characters." –*The LA Times* "This is probably Margulies' best play to date ..." –*The NY Post* "... always fluid and lively, the play is thick with ideas, like a stock-pot of good stew." –*The Village Voice* [2W] ISBN: 0-8222-1640-X

★ **FREEDOMLAND by Amy Freed.** An overdue showdown between a son and his father sets off fireworks that illuminate the neurosis, rage and anxiety of one family – and of America at the turn of the millennium. "FREEDOMLAND's more obvious links are to *Buried Child* and *Bosoms and Neglect*. Freed, like Guare, is an inspired wordsmith with a gift for surreal touches in situations grounded in familiar and real territory." –*Curtain Up* [3M, 4W] ISBN: 0-8222-1719-8

★ **STOP KISS by Diana Son.** A poignant and funny play about the ways, both sudden and slow, that lives can change irrevocably. "There's so much that is vital and exciting about STOP KISS ... you want to embrace this young author and cheer her onto other works ... the writing on display here is funny and credible ... you also will be charmed by its heartfelt characters and up-to-the-minute humor." –*The NY Daily News* "... irresistibly exciting ... a sweet, sad, and enchantingly sincere play." –*The NY Times* [3M, 3W] ISBN: 0-8222-1731-7

★ **THREE DAYS OF RAIN by Richard Greenberg.** The sins of fathers and mothers make for a bittersweet elegy in this poignant and revealing drama. "... a work so perfectly judged it heralds the arrival of a major playwright ... Greenberg is extraordinary." –*The NY Daily News* "Greenberg's play is filled with graceful passages that are by turns melancholy, harrowing, and often, quite funny." –*Variety* [2M, 1W] ISBN: 0-8222-1676-0

★ **THE WEIR by Conor McPherson.** In a bar in rural Ireland, the local men swap spooky stories in an attempt to impress a young woman from Dublin who recently moved into a nearby "haunted" house. However, the tables are soon turned when she spins a yarn of her own. "You shed all sense of time at this beautiful and devious new play." –*The NY Times* "Sheer theatrical magic. I have rarely been so convinced that I have just seen a modern classic. Tremendous." –*The London Daily Telegraph* [4M, 1W] ISBN: 0-8222-1706-6

DRAMATISTS PLAY SERVICE, INC.
440 Park Avenue South, New York, NY 10016 212-683-8960 Fax 212-213-1539
postmaster@dramatists.com www.dramatists.com